# Japanese pure and simple

Kimiko Barber

# Japanese
# pure and simple

photography by Jan Baldwin

Kyle Cathie Limited

*To Stephen, my husband, lover, father of our boys, Maxi, Frederick and Dominic, advisor and most of all, best friend*

*To Mrs Junko Ohtaki and her young doctor son, Yuhei Ohtaki*

# Contents

## Cooking in Japan

## The dishes

## How to eat

All recipes serve 4, unless otherwise stated

# Introduction

**I love food**. Above all, I am a passionate home cook; I love sharing the food I've cooked with my family and friends. I believe that the food I love and grew up with has kept us all happy and healthy. In this book I want to extend my passion for Japanese home cooking to you to share with your own family and friends.

Every culture has its own unique history of food and cooking, and Japanese cuisine is no exception – it has a long, deep-rooted and rich history. A nation's cuisine occupies a more important position than is often perceived but, above all, it has a profound effect on the nation's health. Today, more than at any other time in recent history, there is a heightened awareness of food and health. Hardly a week passes by without another finding or warning, with bewildering, not to mention downright confusing, claims and counterclaims about what to eat, what not to eat and how to eat. Furthermore there is no end to new fashionable 'diets', adding to our fear and confusion. We are bombarded with 'information' on food. All this is turning the pleasure of eating into something we feel guilty about. I want to stop that and take you back to the simple pleasure of home cooking and home entertaining because I know that healthy eating starts at home.

I was born in the mid 50s in Kobe in Japan where I grew up until I left for England in the early 70s. I was fifteen when I arrived at boarding school. I loved my school but the food made me very homesick. My least favourite dishes were rice pudding and over-cooked vegetables that had lost their goodness, nutrition, taste, texture, colours and flavours; in other words, their integrity. How I longed for my mother's and grandmothers' cooking – authentic Japanese home food. During my first term at school, I lost so much weight my mother did not recognise me when I met her at Tokyo airport. I had become disenchanted with school food and had developed an unhealthy attitude towards food. Thank goodness, I returned home to my mother and three grand-mothers who were all passionate cooks. During that Christmas and New Year holiday, I went back into their kitchens and we cooked together. Even simple tasks like washing and chopping seasonal vegetables felt worthwhile and deeply satisfying. The happy ending to this story is that I regained my love of food and my passion for good home cooking that has never left me.

It gives me great pleasure to see that there are over 100 Japanese restaurants in London alone and many more are thriving all over Britain today. Many chefs, both Japanese and non-Japanese, stretching from New York to Sidney, are creating exciting cutting-edge food that puts Japanese cuisine in the mainstream of world cuisine. It fills me with even greater pleasure to see that locals are filling the restaurants once kept in business by homesick Japanese businessmen and tourists. Many Japanese ingredients, formerly regarded as strange and hard to find, are now readily available on supermarket shelves. Furthermore, increasing numbers of British farmers are growing Asian vegetables, which are becoming available in supermarkets.

Thirty years ago, when I first arrived in England as a teenager, it was beyond my wildest dreams to see packed sushi lunch boxes on sale next to sandwiches on supermarket shelves. How things have changed. However, compared to more 'established' Asian cuisines such as Chinese and Indian, Japanese food is still a relatively new arrival and is yet to make itself at home in most Western home kitchens. Japanese food to many people is still shrouded in mystery and seen as a difficult style of cooking. It is my mission to dispel these mysteries and bring Japanese food into everyone's home kitchen. It is a simple fact that restaurant chefs and home cooks are catering for two different audiences – chefs are expected to excel, they are trained, have access to well-equipped professional kitchens with staff and a wide range of ingredients; home cooks aim to nourish their family and friends and keep them well fed, happy and healthy.

As palates become more adventurous and sophisticated, informed diners are seeking food that is not only tasty but also healthy. They want food that is low-fat, low-cholesterol, less dependent on meat and dairy products and more on vegetables and fish. In fact, the Japanese way of eating is exactly how modern Westerners are trying to eat today.

It is well known that Japanese men and women have the longest life expectancy in the world. Japan has the lowest incidence of heart-related disease among developed nations. Obesity is almost unheard of yet (I say 'yet' because Japanese eating habits are rapidly changing) and, with the exception of Sumo wrestlers, it is hard to spot a fat person. Although the evidence is still tentative, there is a number of researches that link the low incidence of menopausal symptoms among Japanese women with a soy protein-based diet. Breast cancer is also rare. I am not suggesting that you should radically change your diet to Japanese food alone, but I invite you to explore the Japanese way of cooking and eating because it is delicious, healthy and surprisingly easy.

## The philosophy of Japanese cooking

In Japanese the word *washoku* is used to distinguish Japanese food from foreign-inspired food, known as *yoshoku*. It is no coincidence that the character *wa* represents peace, harmony and softness. The philosophy of *washoku* is encapsulated by the five principles – five colours, five tastes, five ways of cooking, five senses and five outlooks. The first three principles cover the practical elements of meal preparation, while the fourth principle defines the sensual elements of food; that is, that food must appeal to all five senses, not just taste and smell. The final principle is more spiritual; it requires us to respect and appreciate human endeavour and the forces of nature that provide for us.

**The five colours, *go shiki*,** preaches that every meal should have five colours: white, red, yellow, green and black (including dark colours like purple and brown) to achieve a nutritious diet.

**The five tastes, *go mi*,** means that a meal should contain a harmonious balance of saltiness, sourness, sweetness, bitterness and *umami* to stimulate, but never to overwhelm, the palate.

**The five cooking methods, *go hoo*,** urges cooks to use a variety of different ways of preparing foods: simmering, grilling and steaming being the most common as well as frying and *aemono* (the best translation is 'cooked salads').

**The five senses, *go kan*,** must be stimulated, so not only taste, but smell, sight, sound and touch. In fact, taste is the last element of the five senses, while sight, or a visually pleasing presentation, is an important part of a meal. We have a saying in Japanese that 'we eat with our eyes'.

**The five outlooks, *go kan mon*,** are rules concerned with the partaking of food, and stem from Buddhism, especially the demanding Zen sect where monks observe a strict vegetarian diet of *shojin ryori*. In Zen Buddhism the preparation and eating of food are an important part of the training. First, they instruct us to respect and be grateful for the efforts of all those who contributed to growing and preparing the food. Second, we must do good deeds worthy of receiving food. Third, we must come to the table in peace. Fourth, we should eat food for spiritual nourishment as well as physical well-being. Fifth, we must be earnest in our struggle to attain spiritual enlightenment.

***Umami*** is the fifth sense of taste after salty, sour, sweet and bitter. The flavour of food is determined by a number of different factors including taste, smell, colour, texture, temperature, overall appearance and our memory as well as by physiological or psychological conditions. We all have tasted it and know it but do not know exactly how to put it into words. There is no direct translation in English but in Japanese it is called *umami*, which literally means deliciousness. *Umami* itself is a subtle savoury taste imparted by glutamate and ribonucleotide, including inosinate and guanylate, which occur naturally in many foods such as meat, fish, vegetables and dairy products. A Japanese professor, Kikunae Ikeda, discovered it in 1907. He knew that there is a taste which is common to mushrooms, tomatoes, cheese and meat but which is not one of the four well-known tastes. He developed a method of extracting *umami* by using a large quantity of konbu (kelp seaweed) broth. He managed to extract crystals of glutamate acid, an amino acid that is a building block of protein with a flavour unlike that of the other four tastes. One hundred grams of dried konbu contains about 1g of *umami*.

## Echoing the four seasons

In Japan, the five principles of Japanese cooking are bound up with nature, they include both indigenous Shinto belief and Buddhism and have evolved into a widely encompassing, deeply integrated culinary culture. I often struggle to find an exact word in English to describe Japanese cuisine; in Japanese it is best summed up by the word *shun*, a point in time when a particular food is at its best in taste and flavour. *Shun* can last for several weeks or even months – or it can be a fleeting moment. Although nowadays it is possible to buy almost any ingredient at any time of year, Japanese cuisine, more than any other, respects and appreciates seasonal cycles and other rhythms of nature. And so both professional and home cooks try to echo nature's way of providing us food. Vegetables and fish have their own *shun* when they taste best and are often the most economical. As you would expect, cooking methods and presentation should also reflect the four seasons.

## Alphabet of Japanese seasoning

The Japanese alphabet is made up of a series of consonants followed by vowels. For example, the way to express the 's' characters is *sa, shi, su, se, so*. This third line of our 51 member syllabary also happens to relate to the seasonings used in Japanese cooking. The text below shows the exact order in which seasonings are applied to dishes, based on scientifically proven logic. The principle is that bigger particles, such as those of sugar, cannot penetrate foods when obstructed by smaller particles, such as those of salt. So the following seasonings should always be used in the correct sequence, as shown below:

**Sa** stands for *sato*, which is sugar and sake. Sugar is widely used in marinades and sauces. Sake is used to soften an ingredient or to rid it of odours.

**Shi** stands for *shio*, which is salt. If salt is applied too early, it tightens the cell structure of an ingredient and makes it more difficult to cook, so it must be added at the correct time.

**Su** stands for the same-sounding word *su*, which is vinegar. Vinegar evaporates when heated and loses its flavour, so it is vital that it is not added at too early or too late a stage of cooking.

**Se** stands for *seuyu* or *shoyu*, which is soy sauce. Soy sauce is one of the most important seasoning ingredients of Japanese cuisine. It is added near the end of cooking and is also used for dipping to preserve its unique taste, flavour and aroma.

**So** stands for miso. Like soy sauce, this is used to impart added flavour to many dishes.

If all these sound difficult and strange notions to grasp, there is no need to be disheartened, because most young Japanese today would struggle to articulate the *washoku* philosophy, let alone describe the set of five principles. Perhaps they do not discuss the guidelines for preparing a nutritiously well-balanced, aesthetically pleasing meal. Yet, when it comes to choosing items from a restaurant menu, selecting ready-prepared food from deli counters or buying prepared food from a supermarket only to take it home and reheat in a microwave, most Japanese people, by instinct, employ the five principles to achieve a culinary harmony. It is in our blood.

Selecting ingredients at their best, buying locally available food from both the land and the sea, engaging all the five senses, using a collage of colours, using different methods of cooking, the presenting and serving – the *washoku* approach to cooking provides the opportunity to be creative in every sense, to satisfy your own aesthetic yearnings while providing nourishment and sensory pleasure to family and friends. With this book I hereby extend my invitation to Japanese home cooking.

# Japanese pantry

### Bonito fish flakes – *katsuo bushi*
Together with konbu, this is one of the essential components of dashi or Japanese stock. Traditionally rock-hard, dried bonito fish was shaved just before use, but today ready-shaved flakes available in plastic bags are most commonly used both for preparing dashi and for garnishing.

### Dried shiitake mushrooms
Shiitake are Japan's most popular mushrooms. The dried variety has a stronger taste and aroma and is used as a flavouring ingredient for many dishes.

### Japanese green horseradish – *wasabi*
Wasabi is a perennial aquatic plant. Outside Japan it comes most commonly in paste or powder forms. It is used as a condiment and seasoning.

### Japanese pepper – *sansho*
Sansho is a low-growing, prickly, deciduous bush that belongs to the tangerine family. Almost every part of the tree is used for home-remedies, garnishing and seasoning. Sansho powder, which is made of the ground seedpods, is available in small bottles and has a refreshing peppery flavour and aroma.

### Japanese seven-spice seasoning – *shichimi togarashi*
A mixture of several different spices and flavourings, containing sansho, ground red chillies, hemp seeds, dried tangerine peel, ground nori, black and white sesame seeds and white poppy seeds. Sold in small bottles in Japanese food stores.

### Kelp seaweed – *konbu*
The most important seaweed used in Japanese cooking, konbu is an essential ingredient for making dashi stock. Sold in packets, it has a dark green-black colour, often with whitish patches from dried sea salt. Wipe it clean with a damp cloth but do not soak before using, unless stated.

## Noodles

In this book three basic types of noodles are used. Udon noodles, which are made of white flour, come in various widths and in either flat or in thick strands. They are sold either dried or semi-cooked in vacuum packs. Somen noodles are also made of wheat, but are very fine and sold in dried form. Soba noodles are made of buckwheat flour and commonly light or medium brown. The green variety contains powdered green tea. Both varieties are sold in dried form.

## Sesame seeds – *goma*

Both black and white sesame seeds, the latter more common, are used for seasoning and garnishing. White sesame seeds are toasted and ground to make a paste. You can buy them ready-toasted from Japanese food stores. Middle Eastern tahina or smooth peanut butter are good substitutes.

## Pickled ginger – *gari* or *beni shoga*

Gari is a pale pink pickled ginger used for sushi and as a palate cleanser. It is sold in jars or plastic bags. Bright red beni shoga is used for garnishing.

## Pickled plums – *umeboshi*

Salty pickled plums are a dull red colour and have a fruity fragrance. They are a popular accompaniment for plain boiled rice as they prevent the rice from spoiling. They should be refrigerated after opening.

## Potato starch – *katakuri-ko*

Originally the flour was made of the dried root of *Erythronium japonicum* – dogtooth violet, a perennial plant, which belongs to the lily family. Because of this plant's scarcity, today *katakuri-ko* is mostly made of potato flour and is used as a thickening agent and for coating food before frying. Regular cornflour is a fine substitute.

## Yuzu

This is a Japanese citrus fruit that resembles a tangerine. Its peel and juice are both highly prized and used as seasoning ingredients. It has a refreshing minty taste and pleasant aroma. The juice is available in bottles from Japanese food stores.

# Essential seasonings

These five seasoning ingredients provide essential Japanese tastes and flavours. I strongly suggest you get all of them. They are now available from larger supermarkets, or at least the first four are and substitute mirin with sake and added sugar.

## Soy sauce

Soy sauce is undisputedly the most famous and most widely used seasoning in Japanese cooking. It is made of fermented soya beans, wheat, salt and water. It has a pleasant nutty aroma with a slightly sweet taste. Outside Japan, you are likely to come across three varieties: dark, light and tamari. The dark variety is the most versatile and popular. It is used for marinating, dressing, cooking and dipping. If you are buying just one variety, choose this one. Light soy sauce is surprisingly saltier than the dark and is used mainly in cooking where the intention is not to discolour the ingredients. Tamari in the strict sense should be made without wheat; however, as the term is used loosely by manufacturers nowadays you should read the label carefully if you have a wheat intolerance. Tamari is slightly thicker and sweeter in taste than dark soy sauce and is mainly used for dipping.

## Miso

Miso paste and soy sauce are the two most important seasoning ingredients in Japanese cooking and they share the same origin (fermented soya beans), though miso is the older brother of the two. Miso may contain a variety of grains, including barley and wheat, while the most popular type consists of soya beans mixed with rice culture. Miso comes in a range of colours from light cream *shiro miso* to near-black *haccho miso*. In general, the lighter the colour of miso paste, the less salty in taste. My suggestion in choosing miso is to start with a medium-coloured (like milk chocolate) variety and later add lighter and darker types and blend them to suit your taste. Miso is a very healthy food, packed with vitamin E and minerals, and offers easily digestible protein – soya protein

converted into amino acid. Miso lowers cholesterol, helps to reduce blood pressure and is anti-carcinogenic. The easiest way to use it is to dilute it with dashi stock to make soup or to season simmered dishes. It makes an excellent marinade, good dressing and a wide range of sauces and dips.

## Rice vinegar

Japanese rice vinegar-making developed during the mid-seventeenth century with the fast-growing sake brewing industry. Rice vinegar is a light bronze colour, has a pleasant aroma and is mildly sour but not as sharp as wine vinegar or malt vinegar. One of the hardest working ingredients in the Japanese kitchen, it sterilises, preserves and acts as a natural antiseptic; it is also used to neutralise fishy odours, reduce saltiness and tenderise meat. It refreshes the colour of cooked vegetables and a small amount added in the middle of cooking highlights the flavour of many simmered dishes. Japanese rice vinegar is increasingly easy to find, but cider vinegar makes a good substitute.

## Sake

Sake is Japan's most traditional alcohol beverage. Although it has long since lost its dominance as a mealtime drink to beer and, more recently, wine, its culinary and cultural importance still remains. As a seasoning ingredient, sake adds flavour and depth to many dishes. It is also used to preserve, marinate and to neutralise the strong odour of fish and meat.

## Mirin

Mirin is a sweet cooking sake. It is a light amber-coloured liquid with a slightly syrupy consistency and a mild sake aroma and tastes like a very sweet sake. Mirin is used purely for cooking; it adds sweetness and puts a glossy shine on foods. Out of five essential seasoning ingredients, mirin is the least known and perhaps the most difficult to find – sake and sugar make a good substitute, at a ratio of 1 teaspoon of sugar to 3 teaspoons of sake.

# Essential utensils

### About knives

The most important cooking utensil in the Japanese kitchen is the knife. A Japanese chef's knives are as precious to him as the long and short sword are to a samurai warrior. The spirit of the ancient craft of Japanese sword-making lives on, only it is used to forge kitchen knives made of superior-quality carbon steel. Carbon-steel knives require more care and attention than other types to maintain their hair-splitting sharpness. They should be sharpened regularly by hand with a whetstone but never with a steel knife sharpener or grinding wheel. For a home cook, I suggest buying one stainless-steel kitchen knife that fits well in your hand and looking after it. You are more likely to injure yourself with a blunt knife, as it requires more effort. Do not put it in the dishwasher, but wash it by hand and dry it properly

before storing it. Do not store it in a drawer where other kitchen utensils are kept that might chip or blunt the blade as they touch each other. If you have a knife block, turn the knife on its back to slide it in. In other words, try to minimise the blade coming into contact with hard objects other than food. In Japanese cuisine, preparation, especially cutting, is as important a stage as the actual cooking and it is a pleasurable experience with a sharp knife.

### Cooking chopsticks

These chopsticks are longer than the eating variety and are used for cooking and serving. I personally cannot cook without them in my hand – they are like an extension of my fingers. But if you are not accustomed to using chopsticks, use tongs or a wooden spoon instead.

### Japanese pestle and mortar

After my kitchen knives, the *suribachi* and *surikogi* are the second hardest-working utensils in my kitchen. They are used for grinding or blending ingredients like miso pastes. A Japanese mortar has a serrated inside that makes it easier to grind food.

### Bamboo rolling mat

This is used to roll Japanese omelettes or sushi rolls. It is also used for rolling and squeezing excess water from boiled vegetables such as spinach.

### Earthenware casserole

This is used for the wide range of hotpot dishes that are cooked at the table and for cooking rice. It spreads the heat gently and evenly. There are myriad designs, shapes and sizes of *do-nabe* to suit the wide range of hotpot dishes. A fondue pot or cast-iron casserole dish makes a good substitute.

### Grater

As well as the universal flat grater, there is another uniquely Japanese type: a grater sitting on its own shallow dish to collect both the juice and the grated vegetable.

# Cutting vegetables

Preparation of food is elevated to a fine art form in Japanese cuisine, with cutting vegetables playing a major role. According to each dish and the cooking method, a cook selects the way of cutting the ingredient that is most appropriate, visually pleasing and easy to eat with chopsticks. Here are a few of the basic cuts for preparation and presentation.

*Cutting off skin*

*Round slices*

*Matchstick-sized pieces*

*Rolling cuts*

*Gingko-leaf slices*

*Shavings*

*Angled slices*

*Threads*

# Dashi – the basic flavour

The classic Japanese dashi stock made of seaweed and dried fish flakes takes only 15 minutes to make. It is so simple. So why dedicate a special section to a mere stock, you may well ask? This is because dashi is more than just stock for soups and stews; in the context of Japanese cooking, it provides the backbone to the whole of the cuisine – it is the basic flavour. Dashi gives a subtle undertone to soups, simmered, steamed, stewed dishes, salads, dipping sauces, rice and noodles and wholesome hotpots – it is used everywhere. Once you have mastered the basics of dashi-making, you have laid the foundations of Japanese cooking and the rest will follow.

There are many dashi stock recipes using different ingredients, often involving rather convoluted methods, but there are only three basic dashi stocks you need to know and here they are.

## Vegetarian dashi

This is a subtle and gentle vegetarian dashi using konbu and dried shiitake mushrooms.

2 postcard-sized pieces of konbu
  (kelp seaweed)
3 dried shiitake mushrooms
1 litre water

Soak the konbu and shiitake mushrooms in the water for 1 hour before placing over a low/moderate heat. Slowly bring the water to the boil, but do not let it come to a full boil, and take out the konbu pieces when they begin to float. Increase the heat to boil rapidly for 2 minutes and then turn off the heat. Let the liquid cool before taking out the shiitake mushrooms.

## Mizu dashi – cheat's version

A good cook uses her/his time wisely and plans ahead. And what could be a better way to make flavoursome dashi stock than while you sleep. Although this is called the 'cheat's version' you shouldn't need to feel guilty because this is how millions of Japanese housewives organise their family meals for the following day.

2 litres warm water, (boiled or
  bottled)
1 postcard-sized piece of konbu
  (kelp seaweed)
3 dried shiitake mushrooms
5g dried bonito flakes

Put all the ingredients in a heat-resistant glass jar overnight to infuse. The bonito flakes will have settled to the bottom, but strain before use. It will keep for up to 3 days in the fridge.

# Number one dashi stock

This is the most popular variety of dashi. In Japanese it is described as 'an extracted juice' and I think it is an apt interpretation. Japan is a series of islands surrounded by sea, so it is not surprising that the main building block of its cuisine is made with two marine ingredients: konbu (kelp seaweed) and bonito fish flakes. Good dashi is delicious enough to eat on its own – it is fragrant and subtle yet never fails to ignite a pilot light in me to start cooking! The smell of dashi drifting from the kitchen always reminds me of the beginning of cooking as it was the first thing my mother and grandmothers prepared before anything else. I have tried and tested many different ways of making the number one dashi and come up with this method that is not the quickest but is the easiest and most reliable.

*1 postcard-sized piece of konbu (kelp seaweed)*
*1 litre water*
*20g dried bonito flakes (roughly a handful)*

Soak the konbu in the measured water in a saucepan for at least 30 minutes (ideally 1 hour) before placing it over a moderate heat. If you have not had long enough to soak the konbu, lower the heat to low/moderate to allow more time for the konbu to infuse the water.

Take out the konbu when it begins to float and a few small bubbles start to appear. Pour in a ladle of cold water followed by the bonito flakes. Turn up the heat slightly and cook until the liquid returns to the boil, but do not let it come to a full boil; turn off the heat. Let the bonito flakes settle to the bottom and strain the dashi through a fine sieve lined with a piece of kitchen paper.

**Cook's tip**

Although it requires a little forward planning for the soaking, the actual cooking takes less than 15 minutes – the result is well worth the effort and indisputably superior to shop-bought instant dashi granules that are too salty and often contain monosodium glutamate. I recommend using the dashi stock within the same day of making.

# soups

**Soups** occupy a unique position in Japanese cuisine. Soup is the only dish that appears twice in a meal. At elaborate *kaiseki* meals with seven, eleven or even fifteen courses, two varieties of soup are served, at each end of the meal. To whet your appetite a bowl of delicate clear soup appears at the early stage, while a flavoursome miso soup is served with a bowl of rice and pickles to signal the meal's end. It is often said that the culinary skills of a chef are judged by the taste, aroma and appearance of their clear soup.

At the modest end of the spectrum, a bowl of soup is one of the holy trinity of Japanese cuisine.

The simplest and the most quintessential Japanese meal consists of a bowl of soup and a dish of vegetables (that is often no more than a small plate of pickles) to accompany the main course of a bowl of rice.

Soup plays an important role in the home kitchen – it is easy to prepare, especially once you have mastered dashi stock, and is nourishing and easy to digest.

This chapter has three varieties of soup: dashi-based clear soups, wholesome miso soups and thick soups that may feel more familiar to western cooks but have a Japanese twist.

# Shredded chicken in dashi broth

This simple soup sums up what this book is about – easy, tasty and healthy eating. As the cooking is simple, the ingredients speak for themselves and there is no disguising them, so try to use the best-quality ingredients possible. Use konbu (kelp seaweed) and shiitake mushrooms to take away the smell of the chicken and to add umami (the fifth primary taste) to the soup.

1 lemon, cut into thick slices
2 free-range organic chicken legs
1.2 litres water
2 onions, halved
1 carrot, halved lengthways
1 celery stick
1 garlic clove, slightly bruised by
    the blade of a knife
1 postcard-sized piece of konbu
    (kelp seaweed)
1 dried shiitake mushroom
1 teaspoon rice vinegar
salt and black pepper

Place the lemon slices and chicken legs in a saucepan of water and bring to the boil over a moderate heat. Reduce the heat to low and simmer for 10 minutes before removing the chicken. Rinse the chicken legs under cold running water and pat them dry with kitchen paper. Squeeze the lemon slices in your hand over the chicken.

In a large saucepan, put in the measured water, the chicken and all the other ingredients, except the rice vinegar, and bring to the boil over a moderate heat. Reduce the heat to low and simmer for 30 minutes, skimming off any scum that floats to the surface. Remove and discard all the ingredients except the chicken. Let the broth simmer for a further 10 minutes and adjust the seasoning with salt and pepper before turning off the heat. Leave the chicken in and let it cool down to room temperature.

Remove the skin from the chicken and shred the meat with a fork. If you are keeping the broth for a day or two before serving, add a pinch of salt before storing.

Meanwhile, reheat the broth, add the rice vinegar and adjust the seasoning again. Arrange the shredded chicken in warmed soup dishes. Gently ladle the stock over and serve.

# Kyoto bean soup

This is a Japanese interpretation of Tuscan bean soup. Like its Italian counterpart, this soup is wholesome and nourishing. The addition of miso paste gives a hidden depth without changing the character of the soup. I use a tin of cannellini beans for convenience, but you can substitute any beans of your choice. If you are using dried beans, soak them with three times their volume of water overnight and cook slowly until soft.

1 tablespoon vegetable oil

1 red onion, finely chopped

4–6 rashers unsmoked streaky
  bacon, chopped

1 carrot, roughly chopped
  into chunks

75g burdock, roughly chopped
  and soaked in water

400g Chinese cabbage,
  roughly chopped

4 medium turnips, peeled and
  cut into bite-sized chunks

1.2 litres dashi stock
  (see pages 16–17)

4 tablespoons sake

3–4 tablespoons light soy sauce

200g tinned cannellini beans,
  drained

2 tablespoons medium-coloured
  miso paste

salt to taste

2 spring onions, finely chopped

2 teaspoons toasted
  sesame seeds

Heat the vegetable oil in a large saucepan over a moderate heat and sauté the onion. Add the bacon and cook for 5 minutes before adding all the other vegetables, except the beans, and sauté them until soft. Pour over the dashi stock and season with sake and soy sauce. Bring to the boil, skimming off any scum that floats to the surface. Reduce the heat to low/moderate and add the beans. Allow to simmer for 15 minutes.

Stir in the miso paste gently through a sieve and adjust the seasoning with salt. Ladle into warmed soup dishes. Garnish with the chopped spring onions and sesame seeds and serve.

**Cook's tip**

For a vegetarian recipe, omit the bacon and use vegetarian dashi stock (see page 16).
If you can't find burdock, use celeriac instead.

# Sea bream in clear dashi broth

The Japanese love sea bream. The fish is prized not only for its fine taste and firm texture but also because it is regarded as auspicious. The traditional recipe calls for a cheap cut of fish head but I think using fillets is less scary.

*4 sea bream fillets, skin on,*
 *each weighing 20–30g*
*1¹/₂–2 teaspoons salt*
*1.2 litres dashi stock*
 *(see pages 16–17)*
*2 tablespoons sake*
*4 small pieces (size of a finger*
 *nail) of lime/lemon zest*
*cress*

Place the fillets on a flat basket tray, sprinkle with salt and set aside for 30 minutes. Pour boiling water over the fillets and immediately transfer them to a bowl of ice-cold water (to take away the fishy smell). Put the fillets in a saucepan with the dashi stock and sake and bring to the boil over a moderate heat, skimming off any scum that floats to the surface. Reduce the heat to low and simmer for 5 minutes. Adjust the seasoning with salt. Gently take the fillets out and put them in warmed bowls. Strain the broth and ladle it over the fish. Garnish with the zest and cress and serve.

**Cook's tip**
You can use any white-flesh fish such as cod, plaice, sole or sea bass.
If you don't have a flat basket tray use a strainer lined with kitchen paper.

# Autumn mushroom soup

Japan is a country of seas and mountains. Its mountainous geography and temperate climate provide ideal conditions for mushrooms. And the Japanese make great use of mysterious fungi in their cooking and regularly use 100 different varieties. Shiitake and shimeji are the most popular but others include the elegant enoki, lace-like maitake, slippery nameko and the highly prized fragrant matsutake. I am pleased that more varieties of Japanese mushrooms are becoming available to Western cooks.

4 dried shiitake mushrooms

100ml warm water

1 teaspoon vegetable oil

50g shiitake mushrooms, stalks
  removed and sliced

50g shimeji or oyster
  mushrooms, separated

2 tablespoons sake

2 tablespoons light soy sauce

1.2 litres dashi stock
  (see pages 16-17)

2 teaspoons cornflour mixed
  with 2 tablespoons water

1 free-range egg, lightly beaten

1 teaspoon rice vinegar

salt

2 spring onions, chopped
  diagonally

Rehydrate the dried shiitake mushrooms with the warm water for 15–20 minutes or until the mushrooms become soft. Squeeze out the excess juice and reserve it. Remove the stalks and slice the caps.

Heat the vegetable oil in a saucepan and sauté all the mushrooms for 2–3 minutes, then add the sake and light soy sauce. When the mushrooms become soft, add the reserved mushroom juice and the dashi stock and bring to the boil. Add the cornflour solution and stir well to thicken the soup.

Let the soup return to the boil and pour the beaten egg through a slotted spoon over the soup. Move the spoon as you pour to create a swirling effect. Turn off the heat and let the swirling egg strands rise. Add the rice vinegar. Adjust the seasoning with salt and stir gently. Garnish with the chopped spring onions and serve.

# Vine-ripened tomato soup with red miso

If there is such a thing as a designer miso soup, this is the one. It is a very beautiful-looking dish with a unique and sophisticated taste. I use the most famous red miso, haccho miso, which comes from near Nagoya. It is made of nothing but soya beans and salt, and takes three years to mature. It is almost black in colour and is dry and hard with a slightly bitter taste. If you can't get haccho miso try to use as dark-coloured miso paste as possible.

I make this pesto whenever I have a large amount of coriander. It is wonderful to serve as a condiment for fish or meat or as a pasta or noodle sauce. The pesto keeps for two weeks in a clean glass jam jar in the fridge.

4 medium/large ripe
   vine-ripened tomatoes
1.2 litres vegetarian dashi stock
   (see page 16)
4 tablespoons red miso paste

**for the coriander pesto**
a large handful of fresh
   coriander leaves and stalks
a small handful of fresh
   mint leaves
50g pine nuts
1 teaspoon finely chopped
   lime zest
juice of 1 lime
1 garlic clove
$^{1}/_{2}$–1 teaspoon salt
75ml extra virgin olive oil
$^{1}/_{2}$ teaspoon freshly ground
   black pepper

Blanch the tomatoes in boiling water, peel off the skin and set aside.

Meanwhile, put all the ingredients for the pesto in a blender and process until smooth.

Put the tomatoes in a saucepan with the dashi stock and warm on a gentle heat. With a pestle and mortar grind the miso paste with 1 tablespoon of the dashi stock. Add more stock and keep grinding until the mixture becomes runny enough to pour into the saucepan of dashi stock. Stir in the miso gently and let it return to the boil, then immediately turn off the heat. Place a tomato into the centre of each warmed soup dish or bowl and ladle the soup around it. Do not cover the whole tomato with the soup. Place a small dab of the pesto on top and serve.

**Cook's tip**
You need really ripe tomatoes for this recipe. Let your guests enjoy breaking up their whole tomato with the back of a spoon.

# Aubergine, pork and ginger miso soup

This is a Chinese Ma Po tofu-inspired recipe but using aubergine instead of tofu to get more taste.

1 aubergine
½ tablespoon vegetable oil
1 shallot, finely minced
100g minced pork
25g fresh ginger, peeled and
   finely grated
1 tablespoon soy sauce
1.2 litres dashi stock
   (see pages 16–17)
4–6 tablespoons medium-
   coloured miso paste

Chop the aubergine into small dice and soak them in water for 10 minutes, then drain well – the soaking removes the aubergine's bitterness.

Heat the vegetable oil in a saucepan or wok over a moderate heat, add the minced shallot and sauté until soft. Add the pork and stir-fry for 5 minutes or until the meat is cooked. Add the drained aubergine and grated ginger and stir-fry for another 6–8 minutes; season with soy sauce. Pour in the dashi stock and turn up the heat to bring to the boil, but reduce the heat to low as soon as the stock begins to boil. Put the miso paste in a ladle and gradually dilute it into the soup. Bring the soup back to the boil and then immediately remove from the heat and serve in warmed soup dishes.

**Cook's tip**
If you like a little bit of a kick, add a spoonful of chilli sauce and increase the amount of grated ginger.

# Spring vegetable minestrone with white miso

Millions of Japanese people start and round off their day with a bowl of miso soup. Breakfast miso soups are instantly energy-giving, while a bowl of miso soup at a supper table brings homely comfort. Miso is one of the essential ingredients of Japanese cuisine and features in many different forms, but using it in soups is probably the easiest way.

1/2 tablespoon vegetable oil

1 shallot, finely chopped

50g carrots, diced

50g potatoes, peeled and diced

50g broccoli (preferably
  tenderstem or purple-
  sprouting), roughly chopped

50g spring cabbage, finely
  chopped

50g frozen or fresh garden peas

1 teaspoon salt

100g firm cotton tofu, drained
  (see page 110) and diced

1.2 litres vegetarian dashi stock
  (see page 16)

4 tablespoons white miso paste

1 tablespoon dark-coloured
  miso paste

4 tablespoons cress

Heat the vegetable oil in a large saucepan over a moderate heat. Add the chopped shallot and sweat until soft. Add the rest of the vegetables, sprinkle with salt and sauté until soft. Add the diced tofu, pour in the dashi stock and bring to the boil. Reduce the heat to low and simmer for 5 minutes.

Put the miso pastes in a small sieve and half submerge it in the soup. Dissolve the miso pastes with the back of a spoon into the soup. Bring the soup back to the boil and immediately turn off the heat. Ladle into warmed bowls, garnish with the cress and serve.

**Cook's tip**

There are literally hundreds of varieties of miso paste, but they can be divided into three groups according to the malt ingredients: soya beans, wheat or rice, with the rice malt making up 80 per cent of miso paste produced in Japan. Miso also comes in varying colours, ranging from pale cream to steely dark brown. Colour is a good indication of taste, saltiness and texture. Generally, the darker the colour, the saltier, harder and drier the paste. Buy the medium-coloured variety if you wish to get just one type.

# Tofu and pea vichyssoise with mizuna pesto

Here I have swapped potatoes for tofu – a healthy exchange. This light soup has a wonderful fresh colour and taste of peas. You can serve it warm but it is also delicious chilled for hot summer days.

1 tablespoon vegetable oil

1 tablespoon butter

1 onion, finely chopped

300g frozen or fresh garden peas

2 sprigs of fresh mint

1.2 litres vegetarian dashi stock
   (see page 16)

200g soft silken tofu, drained
   (see page 110) and
   roughly broken

salt

**for the mizuna pesto**

a handful of mizuna or
   rocket leaves, roughly chopped

2 tablespoons pine nuts

zest and juice of 1/2 lemon

1 garlic clove, peeled

2–3 tablespoons extra virgin
   olive oil

1 heaped teaspoon miso paste

salt and black pepper

Heat the vegetable oil and butter in a saucepan over a moderate heat and sweat the chopped onion until soft. Add the peas, mint and dashi stock and bring to the boil. Reduce the heat and simmer for 15 minutes.

Meanwhile, put all the ingredients for the pesto in a blender with 1/2 teaspoon of salt and process until smooth. Adjust the seasoning with salt and a generous amount of freshly ground black pepper.

Add the tofu to the soup and return to the boil. Take the saucepan off the heat, remove the mint leaves and reserve a tablespoon of peas. Blend the soup in a food processor until smooth and adjust the seasoning with salt. If you are serving it warm, return the soup to the saucepan to heat. Drizzle over the pesto, add the reserved peas and serve.

**Cook's tip**

This recipe works equally well with broad beans, but remove the skins before blending to achieve a smooth creamy texture.

# Hokkaido salmon and potato miso soup

This is a hearty, robust miso soup with plenty of substance. The island of Hokkaido was Japan's equivalent of the Wild West – in the late nineteenth century pioneering farmers and miners were encouraged to open up the country's northernmost islands, and this is the kind of soup that would have sustained them.

150g salmon fillet

salt

150g potatoes, peeled

100g carrots, cut into bite-
   sized chunks

150g cabbage, roughly cut

150g leeks, chopped diagonally

1 teaspoon grated garlic

1.2 litres dashi stock
   (see pages 16–17)

2–3 heaped tablespoons
   medium-coloured miso paste

2 spring onions, chopped
   diagonally

Cut the salmon fillet into bite-sized chunks, sprinkle with salt and set aside.

Chop the potatoes into bite-sized cubes and soak in water while you prepare the other vegetables. Drain the potatoes. Put the salmon and all the vegetables in a saucepan with the dashi stock and bring to the boil over a moderate heat. Reduce the heat to low and simmer for 20 minutes, spooning off any scum that floats to the surface.

Put the miso paste in a small bowl and add a ladle of soup to dilute. Add the miso mixture to the soup and stir to blend. Adjust the seasoning with salt if necessary. Let the soup return to the boil and add the chopped spring onions. Turn off the heat and serve in warmed soup dishes.

**Cook's tip**

I often serve this soup garnished with a pinch of chilli flakes and grated ginger – guaranteed to warm up the body and soul on a cold winter night.

# Asian gazpacho with coriander pesto

Gazpacho is the refreshing raw vegetable soup from Spain. This is an equally refreshing and healthy East-meets-West version. Both tomatoes and cucumbers are known to aid digestion and have a cooling effect. It is also a tasty way to encourage fussy eaters to eat raw vegetables.

1 cucumber, peeled, deseeded
  and roughly chopped
500g very ripe tomatoes,
  deseeded and roughly chopped
1 small red onion,
  roughly chopped
1 large red chilli, deseeded and
  roughly chopped
1–2 garlic cloves, peeled
1 tablespoon grated fresh ginger
75ml rice vinegar
juice of 2 limes
2 tablespoons soy sauce
2 tablespoons extra virgin
  olive oil
salt and black pepper
a handful of fresh coriander and
  mint leaves, finely chopped

for the coriander pesto
75g fresh coriander, with roots
50g pine nuts
zest and juice of 1 lime
25g Parmesan cheese, grated
75ml extra virgin olive oil
salt

Put the cucumber, tomatoes, red onion, chilli and garlic in a food processor or a blender and purée. Add the grated ginger, rice vinegar, lime juice, soy sauce and olive oil and purée again. Mix in the chopped coriander and mint leaves. Adjust the seasoning with salt and black pepper and refrigerate for at least 3–4 hours but preferably overnight to allow the flavours to develop.

For the coriander pesto, blend all the ingredients with 1/2 teaspoon of salt until more or less smooth (I personally prefer to have a bit of texture from the pine nuts). Serve the soup in chilled bowls with  drizzles of pesto and olive oil.

**Cook's tip**

It is hard to gauge the amount of chillies as everyone has a different heat tolerance. My advice is to start with less than you think you would like – remember that you can always add more but can't take it out. I also recommend using larger chillies than the small bird's-eye type, which are terribly hot and make the heat level difficult to control.

# Roast pumpkin soup with lime and coriander pesto

This is a visually stunning soup. Roasting not only increases the pumpkin's natural sweetness, but also seems to intensify its vibrant orange colour. My children's favourite way of eating many vegetables is when they are served within a soup and so I recommend you to try it.

1kg ripe pumpkin, peeled, deseeded and cut into wedges

100g elephant garlic (or normal garlic, peeled)

2 tablespoons olive oil

salt and black pepper

1 tablespoon granulated sugar

25g butter

1 medium onion, finely chopped

1.2 litres vegetarian dashi stock (see page 16)

**for the lime and coriander pesto**

zest and juice of 2 limes

100g fresh coriander leaves

1 garlic clove, peeled

salt and black pepper

Preheat the oven to 190°C/375°F/gas mark 5. Brush the pumpkin and garlic with the olive oil and sprinkle with 1 teaspoon of salt and the sugar. Roast in a baking tray for 30 minutes or until soft.

Meanwhile, put all the ingredients for the pesto in a food processor or a blender with $1/2$ teaspoon each of salt and black pepper and process until smooth.

Melt the butter in a saucepan over a low/moderate heat and sweat the chopped onion.

Put the roasted pumpkin, garlic, onion and the dashi stock in a food processor or a blender and purée – work in small batches. Adjust the seasoning with salt and black pepper. Pour the soup into a saucepan to warm up but do not let it boil. Serve in warmed bowls with drops of the pesto in the centre.

**Cook's tip**

This is a warming and comforting soup – serve with crusty wholemeal bread.

# vegetables

**Vegetables** play an important role in Japanese cooking. They are one of the holy trinity of the most quintessential form of a Japanese meal – *ichi ju issai* (literally 'one soup and one vegetable') to accompany a bowl of rice. We eat more vegetables than in the West where the tradition of 'meat and two veg' still seems to live on. In the post-1990s recession era of the early twenty-first century, Japanese consumers have become discerning, demanding more and better-quality seasonal vegetables.

There are many ways of cooking vegetables in Japanese cuisine – raw, pickled, vinegar-flavoured, dressed with other ingredients such as tofu, sesame seeds and miso paste, boiled, steamed, stir-fried, simmered, grilled or deep-fried. Vegetables are treated with the same respect as other ingredients, like fish and meat, in preparing a balanced meal, with taste, colour, nutrition and texture taken into consideration.

One striking feature of Japanese cooking with any ingredients, but especially with vegetables, is the emphasis placed on seasonality. Non-Japanese people may find it almost impossible to understand the passion that a little vegetable can arouse and the trouble some Japanese cooks are prepared to endure in order to secure the season's best offerings, but their efforts will be appreciated at the table. Eating what is in season is the best way for both taste and nutrition and almost always the most economical. I urge you to get to know which seasons are best for which vegetables in your own area and try supporting local growers as much as possible.

These recipes are not necessarily vegetarian but give equal respect to vegetables as to fish or meat. Many of these recipes can be eaten as starters or main courses, not just as side dishes.

# Stir-fry of mangetout and scallops with ginger

I love the Japanese name for mangetout, *kinusaya*, which means silk pod (they are as soft and rubbing them together makes the sound of rustling silk). They are very rich in vitamin C because they are picked while they are still growing. The quick stir-frying method and the addition of scallops make this recipe a great dish for keeping the skin beautiful and aiding recovery from fatigue.

200g mangetout

200g scallops (preferably
  without roe)

3 tablespoons sake

1 tablespoon cornflour

salt and black pepper

1 tablespoon vegetable oil

15g fresh ginger, peeled and
  thinly sliced

75ml dashi stock
  (see pages 16–17)

1 teaspoon rice vinegar

1 teaspoon sesame oil

Remove the strings from the mangetout. Cut the scallops horizontally into two and coat with 1 tablespoon of the sake, the cornflour and a pinch of salt in a bowl.

Heat a wok or large frying pan, add the vegetable oil and sauté the ginger slices to infuse the oil. Add the scallops and stir-fry for 3 minutes. Add the mangetout and cook for a further 3 minutes. Add the dashi stock and bring to the boil, then add the remaining sake, the vinegar and sesame oil and return to the boil before turning off the heat. Adjust the seasoning with salt and pepper and serve.

# Purple-sprouting broccoli with mustard soy

Sprouting broccoli is almost identical to an old Japanese brassica called *nanohana* in its appearance, taste and nutritional value. They are both great health-giving vegetables with high levels of carotene, vitamins B2 and C, and are rich in minerals. They help to develop the body's natural ability to ward off colds, and they help to lower blood pressure, prevent arteriosclerosis, improve the condition of the skin and prevent anaemia. Purple-sprouting broccoli is at its best in late winter and early spring. Do not overcook it as that destroys its valuable vitamin C content.

*400g purple-sprouting broccoli*

**for the mustard soy dressing**
*200ml vegetarian dashi stock*
  *(see page 16)*
*2 teaspoons light soy sauce*
*2 teaspoons mirin*
*2 tablespoons English mustard*
  *powder mixed with*
  *4 tablespoons water*

Trim the broccoli stalks. Bring a large saucepan of salted water to the boil and cook a quarter of the broccoli for 1–2 minutes or until the colour has deepened. Transfer the cooked broccoli on to a flat basket (or use a colander lined with kitchen paper) to drain and fan to cool it down. Repeat the process three more times to cook the rest of the broccoli. (Working in small batches shortens the cooking time and helps to preserve the deep colours of the vegetable.)

When cool enough, gently squeeze the broccoli to rid it of any excess water and lay it on a flat-based dish. Mix all the ingredients for the mustard soy and pour over the broccoli. Leave it for 20 minutes to allow the flavours to develop and then serve at room temperature.

# Japanese spring cabbage coleslaw

There is no doubt that cabbage suffers from bad publicity – the mere mention of the vegetable often provokes dispiriting memories of dull institutional meals. I think this is quite unfair for one of the most accessible and healthy vegetables around. Cabbages have a unique nutrient called vitamin U that is beneficial to the digestive system and prevents fat building in the liver. They are also rich in vitamin C – two or three leaves provide half your daily vitamin C requirement. Here is a delicious, quick and easy recipe to encourage you and your family to eat more cabbage.

200g pointed-head spring
  cabbage
½ medium carrot, peeled
  and cut in fine julienne
200g deep-fried tofu

**for the mustard**
**miso dressing**
1 teaspoon English mustard
  powder, mixed with
  3 teaspoons water
  to a runny consistency
1 teaspoon sugar
2 teaspoons light-coloured
  miso paste
1 tablespoon soy sauce
3 tablespoons vegetarian dashi
  stock (see page 16) or water

Cut away and discard the hard parts of the cabbage and slice it into fine shreds. Blanch the cabbage and carrot for 2–3 minutes and then immediately transfer them to a large bowl of ice-cold water; remove and squeeze them gently to drain off as much water as possible. Meanwhile, heat a frying pan and sauté the deep-fried tofu on both sides. Slice into thin strips when cool enough to handle. Mix all the ingredients for the mustard miso dressing. Put the drained cabbage, carrot and tofu strips in a large bowl and pour over the dressing. Toss gently to coat the mixture and serve.

# Grilled asparagus in dashi

Asparagus was introduced to Japan by the Dutch in the late eighteenth century and was originally grown as an ornamental plant. It is a wonderful vegetable that comes into season in late spring. It's asparagine converts to amino acid when it is digested, which aids a healthy metabolism, energises the body and promotes healthy skin. Green asparagus is more nutritious than the white variety.

*20 asparagus spears*
*2 tablespoons vegetable oil*
*100ml dashi stock*
  *(see pages 16–17)*
*50ml soy sauce*
*25ml mirin*

An asparagus spear has a natural breaking point when you bend it, so break the spears with your hands and discard the hard lower parts. Brush each spear with vegetable oil and grill (or use a ridged grill pan) for 10 minutes, turning them over to cook evenly. Meanwhile, mix the dashi stock, soy sauce and mirin in a flat-based dish. Transfer the cooked asparagus spears to the dish while they are hot to let them absorb the flavour of the dashi mixture and serve.

# Gently simmered bamboo shoots with chicken

My grandfather and I used to go into dew-covered bamboo groves on early spring mornings to dig up young bamboo shoots. I remember having to tread carefully to avoid the tiny shoots whose tips were just pushing through the surface. We used to rush back with a big basketful of them for my grandmother to cook straight away.

100g minced chicken

30g fresh ginger, peeled and
   finely shredded

400g tinned bamboo shoots in
   big chunks, drained

600ml dashi stock
   (see pages 16–17)

3 tablespoons sake

3 tablespoons mirin

pinch of salt

2¹/₂ tablespoons light soy sauce

Heat a saucepan and cook the minced chicken, stirring constantly to prevent sticking.

Divide the ginger shreds into two equal portions and soak one portion in cold water. Add the other half of the ginger, the bamboo shoots and the dashi stock to the chicken and bring to the boil. Reduce the heat and add the rest of the ingredients, except the reserved ginger, and simmer for 10 minutes. Turn off the heat and leave to cool. Serve garnished with the reserved ginger. If you prefer to serve this dish warm, gently reheat it.

# Simmered broad beans with bacon

Like other varieties of bean, broad beans are packed with protein, calcium and other minerals and are rich in vitamin Bs that work to reduce tiredness and prevent hardening of the arteries.

200g broad beans, shelled

2 tablespoons vegetable oil

100g bacon bits

pinch of salt

1 teaspoon sesame oil

**for the cooking liquid**

2 tablespoons sake

1 teaspoon grated fresh ginger

100ml dashi stock
   (see pages 16–17)

1 tablespoon soy sauce

2 teaspoons sugar

Blanch the broad beans for 3 minutes and drain. Heat a wok or frying pan over a moderate heat, add the vegetable oil and sauté the bacon bits. Add all the ingredients for the cooking liquid and cook for 3 minutes, skimming off any scum that floats to the surface.

Turn up the heat to high and add the broad beans to cook for a further 3 minutes. Adjust the seasoning with salt if needed. Add the sesame oil just before you turn off the heat and then serve.

# Avocado dip with wasabi miso

*The Guinness Book of Records* lists avocado as the most nutritious fruit in the world. Although it has double the calories of milk and four times as much fat, it is non-saturated fat, which helps to lower cholesterol. Avocado has nine varieties of vitamins including Bs, C and vitamin E, which work together to slow down the ageing process. It is rich in minerals, especially kalium, which lowers blood pressure, and is high in edible fibre.

2 very ripe avocados

2 teaspoons wasabi powder,
  mixed with 4 teaspoons water

1 teaspoon soy sauce

½ tablespoon medium-coloured
  miso paste

1 teaspoon rice vinegar

Halve the avocados lengthways, twist and discard the stones. Peel the avocados and mash the flesh in a bowl with a fork. Add all the other ingredients and continue to mash until it is well blended into a smooth mixture. Serve with vegetable crudités or breadsticks.

**Cook's tip**
The addition of the rice vinegar helps to maintain the avocado's bright green colour as well as taking a slight edge off the richness. Keep the dip covered with clingfilm until needed.

# Tomato and tofu salad with tomato dressing

A bright red tomato is a symbol of hot summer days. Not only is it beautiful but a highly health-giving vegetable that lowers blood pressure too. It helps you to recover from fatigue and maintains a good digestive system but, most of all, it is known to have anti-carcinogenic properties.

4 tennis-ball-sized ripe
  vine tomatoes

200g soft silken tofu, drained
  (see page 110)

freshly ground black pepper

12 fresh basil leaves, torn

**for the tomato dressing**

2 tennis-ball-sized ripe
  vine tomatoes

1 teaspoon light soy sauce

1 tablespoon extra virgin olive oil

For the tomato dressing, blanch the tomatoes. Skin and deseed them and put them in a food processor with the soy sauce and olive oil. Process for a few seconds or until smooth.

Meanwhile, cut the other tomatoes and tofu block into thick slices and divide into four equal portions. Arrange the tomato and tofu slices on individual plates. Pour the tomato dressing on top and sprinkle with freshly ground black pepper. Garnish with the basil and serve.

# Cucumber and steamed chicken salad with sesame ginger dressing

A cucumber is over ninety per cent water, and its hydrating, diuretic and cooling effects have long been recognised in Chinese medicine. It is best to keep cooking to a minimum to take full advantage of its refreshing taste and texture.

1 chicken breast

pinch of salt

1 tablespoon sake

2 baby cucumbers

½ teaspoon sesame oil

2 spring onions, finely chopped

**for the sesame ginger dressing**

4 tablespoons toasted
sesame seeds

1½ tablespoons sugar

1½ tablespoons rice vinegar

2 tablespoons soy sauce

1 teaspoon peeled, grated
fresh ginger

1 teaspoon medium-coloured
miso paste

Put the chicken breast on a small dish, rub it with salt and pour over the sake. Place it in a steamer and then steam for 10–15 minutes. Set aside to cool.

Meanwhile, cut the cucumbers into wedge-shaped chunks.

For the dressing, use a pestle and mortar to grind the sesame seeds into a coarse paste before adding the rest of the ingredients. Continue to grind to a smooth paste.

Shred the chicken breast with a fork. Put the shredded chicken and cucumber chunks in a large mixing bowl, drizzle over the sesame ginger dressing, add the sesame oil and mix well to coat the chicken and cucumber. Transfer to a serving dish, garnish with the chopped spring onions and serve.

# Stir-fry of red and yellow peppers with beef

This is my adaptation of a traditional Chinese recipe to suit my children, who were less enthusiastic about green peppers and bamboo shoots but preferred red and yellow peppers. Nutritionally, all peppers are rich in the vitamin C that does not break down in the cooking process. Both red and yellow varieties have twice as much vitamin C as the green variety plus a lemon. Vitamin C is good for the skin and helps the body to recover from tiredness.

*1 red pepper*

*1 yellow pepper*

*200g beef fillet*

*2 tablespoons vegetable oil*

*3 tablespoons soy sauce*

*2 tablespoons sake*

*1 teaspoon sugar*

*2 teaspoons oyster sauce*

*freshly ground black pepper*

**for the beef marinade**

*1/3 teaspoon salt*

*1 tablespoon sake*

*1 free-range egg, beaten*

*3 tablespoons cornflour*

Cut the peppers into quarters and remove the seeds and white membrane inside the peppers. Slice into thin strips. Cut the beef into thin strips. Mix all the ingredients for the marinade in a bowl and add the beef to absorb the flavour for 10 minutes.

Heat a wok or frying pan and add the vegetable oil. Stir-fry the peppers for 3 minutes, add the beef and cook for a further 5 minutes. Lower the heat, sprinkle over the sugar and drizzle the soy sauce and sake around the edge of the wok. Add the oyster sauce and season with black pepper and mix well. Turn off the heat and serve.

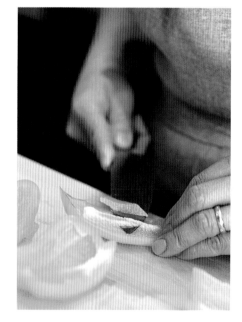 

# Japanese new potato salad with tofu mayonnaise

There is nothing quite like digging up home-grown potatoes from the warm ground on an early summer's day. At this time, before the sun bakes the earth, you can pull out a plant by hand - a dozen or so golf-ball-sized pale new potatoes tumble out. Although the main nutrient in potatoes is carbohydrate, they are rich in vitamins B1 and C (that doesn't break down during cooking) and potassium, which lowers blood pressure, and they also contain plenty of edible fibre. Here is a quick and easy way to enjoy the full taste and nutrients of new potatoes.

*200g new potatoes, washed*
*and scrubbed*

**for the tofu mayonnaise**
*300g tofu*
*½ tablespoon sesame seeds,*
*ground to a smooth paste*
*1½ tablespoons light-coloured*
*miso paste*
*1½ tablespoons sugar*
*1 teaspoon light soy sauce*
*1 teaspoon mirin*
*1 tablespoon rice vinegar*
*pinch of salt*

Drain the tofu (see page 110). You can use either silken soft or firm cotton tofu, but soft tofu has a higher water content and needs longer draining. The drained tofu should be half of its original size and feel solid.

Put the tofu and the other ingredients for the tofu mayonnaise, except the vinegar and salt, in a food processor and process until very smooth. Add the vinegar to blend and adjust the taste with salt if needed. Ideally the tofu mayonnaise should be eaten within a day of making, but can be kept for 3 days in the fridge.

Boil the potatoes in a large saucepan of water until cooked. Let the potatoes cool before coating them with 2–3 tablespoons of the tofu mayonnaise and serve.

**Cook's tip**
It is best not to use too much tofu mayonnaise so that the taste of the potatoes is not obliterated. The creamy mild mayonnaise goes well with practically any cooked vegetables. Try using it as a dip with a difference.

# String beans with sesame miso dressing

String beans are also known as Kenyan or French beans or simply green beans. In the western part of Japan, the beans are sometimes called *sandomame*, which means 'three times beans' because their fast growth allows them to be harvested three times in a year. String beans contain well-balanced B vitamins that help you to recover from fatigue, prevent fat accumulating in the liver and stop the hardening of arteries. Rolling the beans with a small amount of salt on a chopping board keeps the bright green colour after boiling.

*200g fresh string beans*

*1 tablespoon salt*

*1 teaspoon toasted sesame seeds*

**for the sesame miso dressing**

*2 tablespoons toasted*
  *sesame seeds*

*1 teaspoon sugar*

*1 teaspoon light/medium-*
  *coloured miso paste*

*1 tablespoon soy sauce*

Trim the string beans and spread them on a chopping board. Sprinkle over the salt and, with the palms of your hands, roll the beans gently a few times. Bring a saucepan of water to the boil and cook the beans for 3 minutes and then drain well.

Meanwhile, for the dressing, put the sesame seeds in a mortar and grind them to a coarse paste. Add the sugar, miso paste and soy sauce and continue to grind until the mixture becomes smooth and uniform. Transfer the beans to a bowl, add the dressing and mix well to coat the beans. Sprinkle over more sesame seeds to garnish and serve.

# Grilled sweetcorn with teriyaki sauce

Maize is one of the three major grains grown in the world. It is rich in vitamin Bs and E, which work to prevent oxidisation of cells and thereby slow down the ageing process. It is also rich in edible fibre, which prevents constipation and colon cancer.

*4 medium sweetcorn cobs*

*2 tablespoons vegetable oil*

*4 tablespoons teriyaki sauce*
  *(see page 167)*

Cut the cobs into 4cm pieces and cook in boiling water for 10–15 minutes and drain. Brush the cobs with the oil and place them under a hot grill or on a barbecue to cook for 5 minutes or until some parts become golden brown and begin to caramelise. Remove from the heat, brush with the teriyaki sauce and serve.

# Courgettes and tuna chunks with garlic

Every year, I grow a few courgette plants for their flowers and fruit. They are prolific, large, sprawling plants. I have many courgette recipes to use both the flowers and the vegetables. This recipe is one of my family's favourite items on our summer table. Nutritionally, courgettes are a cross between cucumbers and pumpkins – they are rich in carotene, which strengthens the mucous membranes and aids the body's natural resistance.

pinch of salt
200g fresh tuna steak
1 tablespoon vegetable oil
2 garlic cloves, peeled and
  thinly sliced
2–3 medium courgettes,
  cut into thick slices
3 tablespoons soy sauce
1¹/₂ tablespoons rice vinegar
freshly ground black pepper

Sprinkle the salt over the tuna steak and set aside.

Heat a frying pan and add the vegetable oil, reduce the heat to low and cook the sliced garlic until it turns golden yellow and becomes crisp. Remove the garlic slices with a slotted spoon and set aside.

Increase the heat to high and sauté the tuna steak for 1 minute on each side. Remove the steak to a chopping board and let it cool down before cutting it into bite-sized cubes.

Replenish the oil in the pan if necessary and reduce the heat to moderate to cook the courgette slices until they turn golden brown on both sides. Add the tuna cubes and season with the soy sauce and vinegar. Transfer the mixture to a serving plate, sprinkle with the garlic slices, season with black pepper and serve.

**Cook's tip**
I often serve this with cooked pasta as a one-course lunch.

# Spicy edamame

Edamame used to be young soya beans harvested early, until the end of the seventeenth century when special edamame breeds were developed. Like their older brother, edamames are rich in protein, minerals, calcium and vitamin B1 but also in vitamin C, which is absent in soya beans. Edamame also contain a type of amino acid that protects the kidneys and liver from the harmful effects of alcohol. In Japan, edamame are one of the favourite accompaniments for beer. They are in season in the summer when they are sold fresh in their pods, but they are available frozen throughout the year.

*400g fresh or frozen edamame*
*(in pods)*
*2 fresh red chillies*
*2 tablespoons soy sauce*
*2 teaspoons rice vinegar*

Put the edamame and the chillies in a large saucepan of water and bring to the boil. Cook for 3 minutes, scooping out any scum that floats to the surface. Be careful not to overcook the beans. Drain and reserve the chillies. Pour the soy sauce and vinegar over the beans while they are still hot and toss to coat them. Serve either at room temperature or chilled, garnished with the chillies, if you like.

# Stir-fried carrots and deep-fried tofu

Carrots have long been regarded as a warming vegetable that are beneficial to the lungs and spleen, which control blood quality. Their high carotene level converts into vitamin A when it is digested and helps the body's natural immunity as well as having anti-carcinogenic properties.

4 medium carrots, cleaned

2 sheets deep-fried tofu

2 tablespoons vegetable oil

50ml dashi stock (see pages 16–17)

2 tablespoons light soy sauce

2 tablespoons sugar

1 teaspoon sesame oil

2 tablespoons toasted sesame seeds

Cut the carrots into matchstick-sized pieces. Place the deep-fried tofu in a sieve and pour over boiling water to rid it of any excess oil. Cut it into thin strips. Heat a wok or frying pan and add the vegetable oil. Stir-fry the carrots for 3 minutes, then add the dashi stock, soy sauce and sugar. Reduce the heat to low and continue to cook until the liquid has evaporated. Add the sesame oil and stir well before turning off the heat. Sprinkle over the sesame seeds and serve.

# Steamed aubergine with spicy miso dressing

There is an old saying in Japanese that you should not let your daughter-in-law eat an aubergine in autumn. One unkind interpretation is that this is because aubergines are at their best in autumn and a wicked mother-in-law thinks they are too good for her daughter-in-law. But a kinder interpretation is that aubergines have a cooling effect and lower your body temperature.

2 aubergines

**for the spicy miso dressing**

1 garlic clove, peeled and grated

10g fresh ginger, peeled and grated

1 shallot, minced

3 tablespoons soy sauce

1 tablespoon medium-coloured
   miso paste

2 tablespoons rice vinegar

1 tablespoon toasted sesame seeds

1 teaspoon sesame oil

Cut off the aubergine stems and quarter them lengthways. Soak them in water for 10 minutes to rid them of their bitterness. Drain them and pat dry with kitchen paper. Steam the aubergines for 12–15 minutes or until they are soft in the middle. Lay them out flat on a chopping board and fan them to cool down.

Mix all the ingredients for the dressing. Transfer the aubergines to a serving dish, drizzle over the dressing and serve.

**Cook's tip**

Do not refrigerate aubergines as they prefer warmer temperatures and refrigeration hardens the skin.

# Daikon salad with watercress and walnuts

Giant white radish is called daikon in Japanese, which means a big root. Although it is not native to the country, it is the most widely cultivated vegetable in Japan and used extensively in its cuisine. Known as a natural digestive, it is nearly always served with grilled fish. It is rich in vitamins A, C and E, but the health benefits of its vitamin C content can be lost by peeling, cooking and leaving too long after grating. It is also a marvellous natural remedy for a hangover – a cupful of grated daikon should do the trick.

200g daikon (Japanese
  white radish)
pinch of salt
1 tablespoon rice vinegar
50g watercress
6 walnuts, shelled and
  roughly chopped

for the dressing
2 tablespoons rice vinegar
2 tablespoons extra virgin
  olive oil
2 teaspoons grated shallot
2 teaspoons light soy sauce
1 teaspoon sugar
freshly ground black pepper

Cut the daikon into thin slices and then into thin matchstick-sized pieces. Put them in a bowl, sprinkle over the salt and vinegar and set aside for 10 minutes.

Meanwhile, mix all the ingredients for the dressing. Lightly squeeze the daikon to rid it of any excess liquid and mix with the watercress and walnut pieces in a salad bowl. Drizzle over the dressing and serve.

# Shimeji mushrooms and ginkgo nut parcel

Mushroom hunting was one of the seasonal delights of my early childhood. They contain vitamin B2, which lowers cholesterol, and vitamin D that helps the body to absorb calcium. They are rich in edible fibre and have no calories, which makes them an ideal diet food. Shimeji mushrooms are renowned for their flavour: they contain high levels of an amino acid that has umami (the fifth primary taste).

2 packets shimeji mushrooms

4 tablespoons extra virgin
  olive oil

2 garlic cloves, peeled and
  lightly bruised

12 ginkgo nuts (sold ready to use
  in vacuum packs or tins)

$1/2$ teaspoon salt

4 thick slices of lime

4 sheets of A4-sized tinfoil

Preheat the oven to 180°C/350°F/gas mark 4. Cut off the base of the mushrooms and separate them (or if desired keep them in little clumps). Heat a frying pan over a moderate heat and add the olive oil and garlic to infuse. Take the garlic out when it turns golden yellow. Increase the heat and quickly sauté the mushrooms and gingko nuts; season with the salt.

Divide the mushrooms into four equal portions and transfer each portion into the centre of a tinfoil sheet. Add a lime slice to each one and gather the corners in to make parcels. Try to make the parcels as roomy as possible. Put the parcels on a baking tray and bake them for 5 minutes. Serve unopened and let your guests enjoy the fragrance as they open them.

# Roasted sweet potato with soy honey glaze

Sweet potatoes saved the Japanese from a nationwide famine in 1732 and food shortages during the World Wars and immediate post-war periods. The main nutritional component of sweet potatoes is carbohydrate, twice as high as that of ordinary potatoes. They are a high-energy-giving vegetable. They also have stable vitamin C, equivalent to that of grapefruit, which can withstand cooking heat. The sweet potato's edible fibre promotes a healthy colon, prevents constipation and carries cholesterol out of the body to protect against colon cancer and hardening of the arteries. Stone-baked sweet potatoes wrapped in newspaper from street vendors were a popular snack when I was growing up in Japan. It was truly a comfort food. I hope to bring back that sweet memory of my childhood with this recipe. The sweetness increases in the slow roasting.

400g sweet potatoes, peeled
50ml vegetable oil
1 teaspoon sesame oil
pinch of salt

**for the soy honey glaze**
2 tablespoons runny honey
1 tablespoon soy sauce
1 teaspoon juice of grated
   fresh ginger
1 tablespoon toasted
   sesame seeds

Preheat the oven to 180°C/350°F/gas mark 4. Cut the sweet potatoes into ice-cube-sized dice. Put the potatoes in a single layer on a baking tray and drizzle over the vegetable and sesame oils. With your hands, mix the potatoes to coat them with the oils and sprinkle with salt. Place the tray on the middle shelf of the oven and roast for 30–40 minutes or until the edges turn crisp.

Preheat the grill to its highest setting. Mix the honey, soy sauce and ginger juice for the glaze. Drizzle over the potatoes and place under the grill for a further 10 minutes, shaking the tray occasionally. Sprinkle over the sesame seeds and serve.

**Cook's tip**
To extract the juice from grated ginger, simply squeeze it and discard the fibrous remains.

# Cauliflower miso gratin

This is a Japanese version of cauliflower cheese – a soul-warming, comforting dish. Cauliflower has less vitamin C than its green brother, broccoli, when it is raw but they are almost level-pegging when cooked. In other words, cauliflower's vitamin C is heat-resistant and does not break down in cooking, which makes it an ideal health-giving vegetable for the winter.

*200g cauliflower, cut into*
*    small chunks*
*1 medium carrot, cut into*
*    small chunks*
*150g broccoli, cut into*
*    small chunks*
*1 block soft silken tofu, left*
*    wrapped in kitchen paper*
*    to drain*
*25g butter*
*1 tablespoon plain flour*
*100ml semi-skimmed milk*
*100ml vegetarian dashi stock*
*    (see page 16)*
*2 tablespoons miso paste*
*salt and black pepper*
*2 tablespoons grated*
*    Parmesan cheese*

Preheat the oven to 200°C/400°F/gas mark 6. Blanch the cauliflower, carrot and broccoli and set aside to drain. Cut the tofu into bite-sized cubes. Melt the butter in a saucepan and add the flour to make a base for a white sauce. Pour in the milk and dashi and stir. Dilute the miso paste with a little of the sauce and then add it to the pan, stir well and turn off the heat. Adjust the seasoning with salt and pepper. Put the vegetables and tofu in a buttered ovenproof gratin dish and pour over the sauce. Sprinkle over the grated Parmesan and bake for 15–20 minutes.

**Cook's tip**

Add vinegar to the boiling water to keep the cauliflower white. You can use any miso of your choice, but lighter-coloured miso paste is less salty and better suited to this recipe.

# Warm bean sprout salad with crispy garlic

I grow bean sprouts in a large jam jar – it's so easy and quite fun to watch them sprout. Soak a handful of mung beans in water, wash and drain them. Leave the beans in the jar covered by a mesh lid (or buy a growing jar from a health shop) and place it in a sunny spot in the kitchen. Rinse them once a day for the next 2–5 days and you will have fresh home-grown bean sprouts!

200g bean sprouts, roots
  removed
3 tablespoons vegetable oil
1 teaspoon sesame oil
2 garlic cloves, peeled and
  thinly sliced
½ teaspoon chilli flakes
1 tablespoon soy sauce
pinch of salt
1 tablespoon toasted
  sesame seeds

Blanch the bean sprouts in boiling water and drain well. Heat a frying pan over a moderate heat and add both the vegetable and sesame oils. Add the garlic slices and cook until crisp and golden. Remove the garlic slices to a piece of kitchen paper and set aside. Increase the heat to high, add the bean sprouts and toss well to coat each sprout with the oil. Keep this very brief – it is only to heat the sprouts, not to cook them. Add the chilli flakes and soy sauce, adjust the seasoning with salt and turn off the heat. Transfer to a serving dish, sprinkle over the garlic slices and sesame seeds and serve.

# Roast pumpkin and garlic mash

One of my grandmother's pet subjects was how to avoid getting a cold and she believed in eating pumpkin on the winter solstice. It contains plenty of carotene, which converts to vitamin A when it is digested and strengthens the body's natural immunity. It is also rich in vitamins C and E, which prevent hardening of the arteries and slow ageing. On top of all these benefits, it is a truly comforting vegetable with its bright colour, velvety-smooth texture and sweet nutty taste.

500g pumpkin, deseeded and
  cut into 4 equal-sized pieces
4 garlic cloves, peeled
2 tablespoons vegetable oil
salt
½ teaspoon sesame oil
2 tablespoons mirin
1 teaspoon medium-coloured
  miso paste

Preheat the oven to 200°C/400°F/gas mark 6. Put the pumpkin pieces, skin-side down, on a baking tray with the garlic cloves. Brush on the vegetable oil and sprinkle with a pinch of salt. Roast for 45 minutes or until very soft and the edges have become caramelised. When it is cool enough to handle, scoop out the flesh from the skin. Put the pumpkin flesh and garlic in a food processor or blender, add the sesame oil, mirin and miso and process until very smooth. Adjust the seasoning with salt and serve.

# Spicy stir-fried spinach with pancetta

I love spinach – it is easy to grow, easy to cook, has a beautiful, deep green colour and, above all, is very tasty and packed with natural goodness. Spinach has long been recognised as a power-giving vegetable with a high iron content. It is also rich in carotene (which converts into vitamin A, B vitamins and vitamin C). Of all the vegetables, spinach contains the second most betacarotene, after carrots, which is known to have anti-carcinogenic properties. This is absorbed more efficiently if eaten with oil and fat. Spinach's natural season is late autumn and winter when one needs all the natural remedies to stay healthy.

*400g spinach, washed*

*2 tablespoons vegetable oil*

*100g pancetta or bacon bits*

*2 tablespoons medium-coloured*
  *miso paste*

*2 tablespoons sake*

*1 teaspoon red chilli flakes*

Chop the spinach into 1cm pieces. Heat a wok or large frying pan over a moderate heat and add the vegetable oil. Shallow-fry the pancetta or bacon bits until they become crisp. Add the miso paste and cook for 1 minute, then add the spinach and sprinkle over the sake. Quickly toss the spinach to coat it with the cooking juices. Turn off the heat – do not overcook the spinach as the residual heat is sufficient to wilt the leaves. Sprinkle over the chilli flakes and serve.

# Pot au feu of Chinese cabbage and bacon

Chinese cabbage is one of the most popular vegetables used in Japanese cooking. Although it is now available throughout the year, its natural season is winter. It is a valuable source of vitamin C and minerals such as iron, magnesium and kalium. It is used in many hotpots as slow cooking makes it sweet and easy to digest. This recipe is designed to provide a hearty big soup to warm up the body and soul.

400g green streaky bacon,
   preferably rindless
50g fresh ginger, peeled
   and grated
1kg Chinese cabbage, quartered
   lengthways
200ml sake
600ml water
4 tablespoons light soy sauce
1 tablespoon rice vinegar
4 tablespoons spring onions,
   finely chopped

**for the lime condiment**
2 limes
1 garlic clove, peeled
1/2 teaspoon salt

Divide the bacon and grated ginger into four equal portions and subdivide each portion into three. Take a quartered cabbage and insert bacon rashers with a dab of grated ginger between the cabbage leaves. Continue to make bacon layers until you have used up one portion. Tie the cabbage quarter with a piece of cooking string to hold it together. Repeat the process to make three more servings. Place the four cabbage quarters in a large saucepan and add the sake and water. Put the lid on and bring to the boil over a moderate heat. Reduce the heat and simmer for 30 minutes.

Meanwhile, for the lime condiment peel the zest and finely chop it. Halve the limes and extract the juice. Put the lime juice, zest, garlic and salt in a mortar and pound them into a smooth pesto.

Add the soy sauce and rice vinegar to the cabbage soup and keep warm. Take out the cabbage quarters and let them cool before cutting them into big bite-sized pieces. Reheat the soup if necessary. Place the cabbage in individual serving dishes, ladle over the soup, garnish with the chopped spring onions and offer with the lime condiment.

**Cook's tip**
I suggest you serve this with crusty wholemeal bread.

# Leek and carrot mini frittatas

A Japanese chef friend of mine got very exited when he spotted leeks on sale. He mistook them for a variety of Japanese long white spring onions. The two are not the same but make very good alternatives to each other. Leeks have similar nutritional values to onions and garlic – they are warming, improve blood circulation, and prevent tiredness and a stiff back.

2 medium leeks

1 medium carrot, cut into
   matchstick-sized pieces

2 free-range eggs, lightly beaten

4 tablespoons water

4 tablespoons plain flour

2 tablespoons cornflour

1/2 teaspoon salt

2 tablespoons vegetable oil

**for the dipping sauce**

4 tablespoons soy sauce

1 teaspoon sesame oil

2 tablespoons rice vinegar

Trim the leeks, halve lengthways and slice finely. Put the leeks and carrot in a mixing bowl, add the eggs, water, flour, cornflour and salt and mix well.

Heat a large non-stick frying pan and add the vegetable oil. Divide the leek mixture into eight equal portions and, with a tablespoon, drop each portion into the heated frying pan. Cook for 3 minutes, then turn over each small disc to cook on the other side for 2 minutes.

Meanwhile, mix all the ingredients for the dipping sauce and have it ready.

Put the cooked frittatas on a large serving plate with a dish of dipping sauce and serve.

# fresh from the sea

**Surrounded** by sea, Japanese cooks make full and extensive use of the sea's riches in their daily cooking. It is impossible to separate fish from Japanese cuisine. Visitors to Japan can witness the fondness for fish and seafood at the capital's central wholesale food market in Tsukiji and its surrounding neighbourhood. For six days a week, 800 wholesale traders under one roof buy and sell over 500 kinds of some 2000 tonnes of fresh, frozen or processed fish and seafood, generating ¥2 billion (£20 million) worth of business a day. Tsukiji's pre-eminence in the world fish business sums up Japan's fondness for fish – the nation is the world's largest importer of fish and seafood, accounting for half of the global £17 billion trade.

Japanese cooks go shopping every day to buy the freshest fish of the season. These days, however, we inevitably go to the supermarket; there we can find almost any type of fish, ready-filleted, throughout the year. I used to be highly dogmatic about fish farming and tried to eat only wild fish – now I humbly eat my words. Sustainable organic fish farming holds the key to the future.

There is no doubt that eating fish is healthy – it has high-quality protein that is easier to digest than that of meat or poultry. Fish is rich in vitamins including vitamin A, which benefits eyesight and helps to improve the body's natural immune system. Mackerel, herring and plaice are particularly high in vitamin B2 and niacin that help to maintain healthy eyesight, skin and the working of digestive organs. Both fish and shellfish are rich in calcium, iron and other minerals. But the most striking argument for eating more fish lies in the latest findings of an Anglo-American research project on omega-3 fatty acid, found in fish. The research shows that the children of mothers who ate food with a low omega-3 content during their pregnancies had a lower IQ than their peers, found normal social relations harder to deal with, and lacked fine-tuned physical co-ordination. Nobody is suggesting that fixing maternal nutrition now would cure bad behaviour in future and result in a nation of well-coordinated geniuses, but there is increasing evidence that it would help.

In this book, I would like to demystify the Japanese way with fish and demonstrate that it is not all raw sashimi and sushi – far from it. We have so many different means of cooking fish to suit every occasion, ability and, above all, each of the four seasons. I hope to inspire you to cook more fish for your family and friends.

# Grilled sweet miso-marinated cod

Miso is one of the essential ingredients in Japanese cooking. Japanese home cooks make wide use of it not only for its nutritional and health benefits but also for its distinctive taste and aroma. It is healthy and tasty. The marinating transfers miso's aroma and flavour and increases the natural umami (the fifth primary taste) found in the fish. Although the traditional recipe calls for *saikyo miso*, which is a light-coloured mild miso paste produced in the Kyoto area, you can use any light-coloured miso of your choice.

*4 cod or hake fillets, each*
*weighing 110g*
*4 teaspoons sushi ginger for*
*(optional) garnish*

**for the sweet miso marinade**
*200ml sake*
*100g sugar*
*450g light-coloured miso paste*

For the sweet miso marinade, put the sake in a saucepan and bring to the boil to burn off its alcohol for a few minutes, then turn off the heat. Add the sugar and stir to dissolve. Add the miso paste and stir to incorporate and then set aside to cool. Transfer the miso marinade to a flat-based food container with a lid and bury the fish fillets in the marinade. Place the container in the fridge overnight.

Preheat the grill. Wipe the fillets with your fingers or kitchen paper. Do not wash them as it will spoil the taste. The fish should feel firmer. Place the fillets under the grill for 5–7 minutes on one side, until they turn golden, and then grill on the other side for 3–5 minutes. Keep an eye on the fish as it easily burns. Garnish with sushi ginger, if desired, and serve.

**Cook's tip**
The famous Japanese restaurant chain Nobu brought this traditional dish into the limelight with black cod fillet, which is not actually related to cod. You can use any white fish. The miso marinade can be re-used once or twice, depending on its wateriness – reheat it to evaporate the excess water. Do not marinate for longer than overnight as over-marinating makes the fish dehydrated and hard with an overpowering miso taste.
Serve this simply with steamed green beans or, in the summer, a few sprigs of watercress.

# Seared tuna steak with daikon dressing

Tuna is the number one favourite fish of the Japanese. Tsukiji fish market in Tokyo alone trades over 2000 tunas, fresh or frozen, daily and nearly half of the wholesale traders specialise in tuna. Although the nation's favourite way of eating tuna is raw in sashimi or sushi, quickly searing the outside is probably less scary for the home kitchen.

4 tuna steaks, each weighing
  100–120g and 2½ cm thick
1 tablespoon vegetable oil
handful of wild rocket leaves
8 chives, finely chopped

**for the marinade**
100ml soy sauce
50ml sake
2 tablespoons rice vinegar
1 garlic clove, peeled and grated

**for the daikon dressing**
4 tablespoons grated daikon
  (Japanese white radish)
4 teaspoons lemon juice
4 tablespoons soy sauce

Mix all the ingredients for the marinade and marinate the tuna steaks in it for at least 30 minutes. Take the steaks out of the marinade and pat them dry with kitchen paper.

Heat a heavy-based frying pan or, better still, a griddle pan over a moderate heat. Brush the steaks with vegetable oil. Cook on one side for 2 minutes, then turn over and cook the other side for 1–2 minutes.

Meanwhile, for the daikon dressing, mix the daikon with the lemon juice and soy sauce.

Transfer the steaks on to individual serving plates and arrange the dressing and a few rocket leaves over them. Garnish with the chopped chives and serve.

**Cook's tip**
The robust taste of tuna needs an accompaniment that will counterbalance it and I personally find buttery avocado makes a very good partner.

# Simmered sardines in ginger vinegar

Some of you may have noticed by now that I use a lot of vinegar in cooking. Vinegar is a wonderfully tasty and healthy ingredient with a wide range of culinary uses. It takes away the fishy smell of sardines and it tenderises meat, making it easier to digest and absorb.

8 fresh sardines

40g fresh ginger, peeled

1 large red chilli

250ml rice vinegar

200ml sake

75ml soy sauce

2 tablespoons mirin

1 tablespoon sugar

4 heaped tablespoons dried
   wakame (seaweed), soaked
   in water

1 sheet of baking paper cut into
   the same size as the
   saucepan with a few
   small holes

Remove all the fish scales by scraping the blade of a kitchen knife from the tail end to the head. Remove the heads and gut the fish. Rinse them under cold running water and pat dry with kitchen paper. Cut the ginger into small matchstick-sized pieces.

Put the sardines in a large shallow saucepan and add the ginger and all of the other ingredients, except the wakame. Bring to the boil over a moderate heat and then reduce the heat to low as soon as the liquid begins to boil. Simmer, using the baking paper as a lid, for 30 minutes.

Meanwhile, soak the dried wakame seaweed in a large bowl of water for 10 minutes or until soft. Drain, chop it roughly and set aside.

Transfer the sardines to a large serving dish, arrange the ginger over them and drizzle over a few tablespoons of the cooking juices. Add the wakame and serve.

**Cook's tip**
Serve with steamed or lightly boiled broccoli, cauliflower and carrots.

# Salt salmon flakes

In Japan, salmon is rarely eaten fresh but usually salted. A slice of grilled salt salmon is one of the most popular dishes at breakfast, lunch and dinner; in other words, at any time. All my grandmothers used to make their own salt salmon and yellowtail for the New Year holidays when fish markets were closed. I always sensed that another year was drawing to an end and a New Year was approaching when I saw a few big fish hanging under the eaves of the house. I wonder how a little bit of salt and cold winter wind made the fish so tasty that the flavour is still imprinted on my taste buds.

Salt is one of the most important ingredients in Japanese cooking. We use salt to flavour, season, preserve, dehydrate, anti-oxidise and to freshen up the colours of food, so it is a pity that this remarkable ingredient is often misunderstood and seen as a villain of the modern healthy lifestyle. Of course, too much salt on anything is bad for you. But the real villain is what I call 'hidden salt', present in many processed foods, which you have no control over. But in your own kitchen you are in control – this is one of the reasons why I love cooking.

I resumed the family tradition of preparing salt salmon last winter, when I was writing this book. Since then there have always been a few slices of salt salmon and a jar of salmon flakes in my fridge, so that I can make a tasty meal at a moment's notice or the first rumbling of my tummy. Salmon flakes are a great addition to salads or pasta sauces.

## How to make salt salmon

*1 whole side of fresh organic*
  *salmon fillet*
*2 tablespoons sea salt*

Choose a fresh organic salmon. Choosing is always easier if you can see the whole fish as it gives you more clues to its freshness. Pick one which has clear bright eyes, glistening silver skin and bright gills. Above all, it should not smell fishy; fresh fish should smell of the sea but not have an unpleasant odour. Get your fishmonger to fillet the salmon if you can't do it yourself. (Remember: there is no shame in asking – in fact, a good fishmonger will be delighted to do it for you.) Put the fillet on a clean kitchen surface and sprinkle 1 tablespoon of salt over one side, then do the same on the other. Wrap it with triple-layered kitchen paper and place it on a plastic tray lined with a few sheets of newspaper; do not cover it. Refrigerate for 4–5 days.

**Cook's tip**

Salt salmon will keep for a further 7 days in the fridge. Slice and grill it as required.
The method works equally well with other fish such as yellowtail, sea bream (refrigerate for only 2–3 days) and mackerel (for 1–2 days).

## How to make salt salmon flakes

*300g salt salmon (see page 68)*

*3 tablespoons sake*

*1 tablespoon soy sauce*

Boil the salt salmon for 10 minutes. Drain and let it cool enough to handle. Remove the skin and, with your hands, flake it. Put a non-stick frying pan over a moderate heat and add the fish flakes. Stir rapidly with either two pairs of chopsticks or a wooden egg whisk to fluff the fish. Add the sake and soy sauce and continue to cook until nearly all the liquid has evaporated. Let it cool to room temperature before transferring into a glass jar to store in the fridge.

The salt salmon flakes work wonderfully well with cooked soba or udon noodles and pasta. They also make a good salad topping. The more traditional way is to serve them on top of freshly cooked rice.

## Grilled yuzu-marinated turbot with peppers

Yuzu is a highly aromatic Japanese citrus fruit used only in cooking. Outside Japan the juice is available in bottles, but lime juice makes a good substitute.

*4 turbot slices of about 1¹/₂cm*
  *thick, each weighing 100–125g*

*1 green pepper, quartered*

*1 yellow pepper, quartered*

*1 red pepper, quartered*

*1 tablespoon vegetable oil*

**for the yuzu marinade**

*4 tablespoons light soy sauce*

*4 tablespoons sake*

*2 tablespoons yuzu juice or*
  *lime juice*

*2 tablespoons mirin*

Make a criss-cross insertion on each turbot slice to encourage the marinade to soak in. Mix the yuzu marinade ingredients in a shallow dish, add the fish and marinate for 30 minutes.

Preheat the grill and line a baking tray with tinfoil. Brush the quartered peppers with the oil. Place the fish and peppers on the baking tray and grill for 6–8 minutes on one side. Brush the turbot with more marinade and turn over to cook the other side for a further 5–7 minutes. Serve the fish with the peppers.

# Aromatic steamed salmon with shallots and broccoli

I am greatly encouraged by the rising public criticism of intensive fish farming. People have realised that the price of salmon is not the only thing being brought down by intensive fish farming but also the quality of the fish at an immeasurable cost to the environment. There is a growing number of organic salmon farms producing chemical-free fish in more environmentally friendly surroundings. Sustainable organic fish farming must surely hold the key to the future.

400g organic salmon fillet

2 shallots

100g broccoli

2 tablespoons cornflour

**for the aromatic seasoning**

4 tablespoons sake

6 tablespoons soy sauce

2 teaspoons juice of grated
  fresh ginger

1 tablespoon sesame oil

freshly ground black pepper

Cut the salmon into 2.5cm chunks and put them in a bowl.

Mix all the ingredients for the aromatic seasoning and pour the mixture over the salmon. Stir to ensure that each salmon piece is coated with the mixture and set aside for 15 minutes.

Peel the shallots and cut them and the broccoli into bite-sized pieces.

Pat the salmon dry with kitchen paper and dust it with cornflour. Put the vegetables and salmon in a heat-resistant bowl, place in a steamer and steam for 15–18 minutes. Serve on warmed plates with the cooking juices.

**Cook's tip**

Why not serve this with plain boiled or mashed potatoes to soak up all the tasty cooking juices?

# Baked parcels of konbu-flavoured plaice

This is a highly sophisticated and delicious way of presenting a subtle-flavoured fish like plaice or sole with surprisingly little cooking. Umami, found in abundance in konbu (kelp seaweed), transfers to, and intensifies, the delicious taste of the fish, which is wrapped in a parcel so that no taste and flavour is lost. The konbu is made into bows for visual effect.

4 sheets of konbu (kelp
   seaweed), big enough to wrap
   each fish fillet
½ teaspoon salt
4 plaice fillets, each
   weighing 110g
1 teaspoon vegetable oil
4 tablespoons sake
1 lime or lemon, cut into
   4 wedges

Cover the konbu sheets with a clean damp tea cloth for 10 minutes to soften.

Meanwhile, sprinkle salt on the fish fillets and set aside for 5–10 minutes. Take the softened konbu sheets and pat dry with kitchen paper. Use one konbu sheet to wrap each fillet, tightly cover with clingfilm and refrigerate for 2–3 hours.

Preheat the oven to 170°/325°F/gas mark 3. Cut four sheets of tinfoil large enough to envelop the fillets. Unwrap the fillets from the konbu – reserve one sheet and discard the rest.

Cut four ribbons (1cm wide x 7cm long) from the reserved sheet of konbu and tie a knot in the middle of each ribbon. Lightly brush the central part of each tinfoil sheet with vegetable oil and place the fillets on them, add the konbu knots and pour over the sake. Bring up the edges of the tinfoil to make parcels. Put the parcels on a baking tray and place in the middle of the oven to bake for 10–15 minutes. Lay each parcel, unopened, on a plate and serve with a lime or lemon wedge.

**Cook's tip**

You can use any of the flat fish for this recipe. If the fish is fresh sashimi-quality, just do the konbu marinade and serve raw as sashimi.

These parcels require something delicate to accompany them – try some steamed green beans or bok choy.

# Pan-sautéd marlin with citrus teriyaki sauce

The marlin is large and handsome with an impressive bill. Its flesh is a pinkish-orange colour. It is a healthy fish, high in protein and low in fat, but the most notable health-giving element it contains is kalium, which helps to prevent high blood pressure.

4 marlin steaks, each
  weighing 120g
1 tablespoon plain flour
200g shimeji mushrooms
2 tablespoons vegetable oil
150ml water
100g broccoli, cut into
  bite-sized chunks
pinch of shichimi togarashi
  (Japanese seven-spice
  seasoning)

**for the citrus teriyaki sauce**
2 tablespoons medium-coloured
  miso paste
1 tablespoon soy sauce
2 tablespoons sake
1 tablespoon lime juice
1¹/₂ tablespoons sugar

Lightly dust the marlin steaks with the flour. Divide the shimeji mushrooms into four equal portions. Heat a frying pan over a moderate heat and add the vegetable oil. Quickly sauté the marlin steaks on both sides and set them aside. Add the water to the frying pan with the mushrooms and broccoli and cook for 3–4 minutes.

Mix all the ingredients for the citrus teriyaki sauce and have it ready.

Take the vegetables out of the pan with a slotted spoon and keep warm. Add the citrus teriyaki sauce to the pan and return the marlin steaks to cook until the liquid has reduced by 20 per cent. Arrange the fish on individual serving plates, add the vegetables and drizzle over some of the cooking sauce. Garnish with shichimi togarashi and serve.

**Cook's tip**
Although this recipes contains broccoli, it shouldn't stop you adding more chunky cuts of vegetables of your choice.

# Japanese-style sea bass carpaccio

In Japan, sea bass is known as *shusse uo*, meaning 'success fish' because it changes its name as it grows bigger. Sea bass is valued for its firm white flesh and good subtle taste. You need sashimi-quality fresh wild sea bass for this recipe and there is no cooking involved.

200g sashimi-quality wild sea
   bass fillet, skin removed
½ teaspoon salt
2 tablespoons sake
2 tablespoons rice vinegar
1 tablespoon lime juice
1 vine tomato, deseeded and
   finely chopped
8 chives, finely chopped

**for the wasabi miso sauce**
1 tablespoon medium-coloured
   miso paste
1 teaspoon wasabi powder
½ teaspoon sugar
2 tablespoons soy sauce
2 tablespoons water
freshly ground black pepper

With a sharp knife, slice the sea bass fillet as thinly as possible. You will find it easier if you wrap the fillet with clingfilm and semi-freeze it for 10–15 minutes. Lay the slices on a shallow, flat-based dish and sprinkle over the salt, pour over the sake, vinegar and lime juice and refrigerate for 1–2 hours.

Meanwhile, for the wasabi miso sauce, mix all the ingredients together in a bowl and set aside.

Transfer the fish slices on to four individual serving plates. Drizzle over the prepared wasabi miso sauce, garnish with the chopped tomato and chives and serve.

**Cook's tip**

You can try this recipe with other white fish, such as sea bream, plaice or halibut. But make sure the fish is sashimi-quality – in other words, really fresh.
Serve with a bowl of fresh green salad with Japanese salad dressing (see page 169).

# New sashimi of sea bream with hot oil

If tuna is the heavyweight champion fish in the Japanese kitchen, sea bream or snapper is the royal king. Sea bream is a handsome-looking fish with firm pinkish-white flesh and a wonderful flavour. It is also prized as auspicious – it adorns every celebratory table because its Japanese name, *tai*, is a pun on the Japanese word for auspicious. The presence of this fish immediately lights up a table. It is low in fat, high in protein and easy to digest, making it suitable for all ages. This is an easy-to-do, but highly dramatic recipe with an impressive taste and flavour.

250g sashimi-quality sea bream
   fillet, skin removed

1/3 teaspoon salt

1–2 garlic cloves, peeled
   and grated

2 tablespoons lemon juice

1 tablespoon light soy sauce

1 tablespoon rice grains

1/2 teaspoon shichimi togarashi
   (Japanese seven-spice
   seasoning)

**for the hot oil**

2 tablespoons grapeseed oil

1 teaspoon sesame oil

You will find it easier to cut the fish into thin slices if it is wrapped in clingfilm and semi-frozen for 10–15 minutes. Cut the fish fillet into thin slices and arrange the slices on a large serving plate. Sprinkle over the salt and rub the grated garlic on each slice.

Pour over the lemon juice and wait for the fish slices to 'cook' for a few minutes (the colour of the fish turns from translucent to white opaque), then drizzle over the soy sauce.

Meanwhile, dry-toast the rice, grind and set aside.

In a ladle, heat the grapeseed oil and sesame oil until almost smoking. Pour the hot oil mixture over the fish slices. This is a rather dramatic moment, creating a sizzling noise and splashing of oil that semi-cooks the fish. Take care not to burn yourself with the hot oil. Garnish with shichimi togarashi and the ground rice and serve immediately.

**Cook's tip**

If you are preparing this in advance, proceed up to the stage where you heat the oil, then cover the plate with clingfilm and keep refrigerated. The subtle and gentle flavours of young mangetout or steamed green beans will make good partners to this dish.

# Skate wing with wasabi

I first came across the delights of skate wings in England. They are delicious and succulent and easy to eat for those who are not generally comfortable when dealing with fish on the plate. Skate wings can sometimes smell slightly of ammonia, which can be off-putting for some, so I have come up with a recipe that solves this minor problem with a delicious Japanese twist!

2 red onions,

4 skate wings, each weighing about 100–125g

4 tablespoons plain flour

4 tablespoons vegetable oil for shallow-frying

**for the cooking liquid**

4 heaped tablespoons capers

2 tablespoons sake

2 teaspoons wasabi powder

2 tablespoons rice vinegar

Slice the onions as thinly as possible and soak them in a bowl of cold water – this removes the strong onion smell and refreshes them.

Wipe the skate wings clean and dust with flour. Heat a large frying pan over a high heat and add the vegetable oil. Shallow-fry the skate wings for 3–5 minutes on each side or until they turn golden brown and crisp. Reduce the heat to low.

Mix all the ingredients for the cooking liquid in a small bowl, pour it over the skate wings and simmer for 1–2 minutes.

Drain the onion slices. Put the skate wings on individual serving plates, drizzle the cooking liquid over, arrange the drained onion slices on top and serve.

**Cook's tip**

Serve with tomato and tofu salad (see page 40) or Japanese new potato salad (page 44).

# Hot-and-sour vinegar-pickled prawns

Here is an easy, nothing-to-do-at-the-last-minute recipe with plenty of flavour. Both rice vinegar and umeboshi (pickled plums) pickle and preserve the prawns and the vegetables while you sleep. In an ideal world, the prawns should be left at least 24 hours to allow the flavours to develop. A tablespoon of wasabi may sound fiery-hot but gives an undertone of lively heat.

12 cooked giant prawns

1 red pepper, deseeded and very
   thinly sliced lengthways

1 yellow pepper, deseeded and
   very thinly sliced lengthways

1 small red onion, thinly sliced

1 lime, thinly sliced

sprigs of coriander

**for the pickling liquid**

100ml rice vinegar

4 tablespoons yuzu juice or
   lime juice

2 tablespoons light soy sauce

2 umeboshi (pickled plums),
   mashed

1 tablespoon sugar

1 tablespoon wasabi powder,
   mixed with 2 tablespoons
   water

Remove the shells and heads of the prawns but leave the tails on as they look attractive. Run the tip of a small knife along the back of each prawn and remove the black vein that sometimes runs from head to tail. Place the prawns, sliced peppers, onion and lime in a shallow glass or plastic container with a lid.

Mix all the ingredients for the pickling liquid and pour over the prawns. Cover the container and chill in the fridge for at least 24 hours – give the contents occasional shakes or stir from time to time to ensure even pickling.

Serve the prawns and the vegetables with coriander leaves and a generous amount of the pickling juice.

**Cook's tip**

Serve with a big bowl of green salad with Japanese salad dressing (see page 169).

# Oyster congee

Oysters are delicious, health-giving seafood, rich in minerals and B vitamins. Like many children, I did not like raw oysters, so my mother used to cook them in soupy rice (*congee*) for my late night snack when I was revising for many exams. A steaming bowl of oyster congee made late-night revision a little more bearable. It is quick to make, deliciously comforting and very easy to digest.

*200g fresh oysters*

*1 tablespoon lime juice*

*1 postcard-sized piece of konbu (kelp seaweed)*

*600ml water*

*400g cold cooked rice (Japanese-style short-grain or brown)*

*2 tablespoons light soy sauce*

*handful of watercress, chopped*

*2 teaspoons grated fresh ginger*

*½ sheet of nori (dried seaweed), torn into small pieces*

Put the oysters in a bowl, pour over the lime juice and set aside.

Put the konbu with the water in a heavy-based saucepan and let it come to the boil over a moderate heat. When the konbu floats to the surface, blanch the oysters in the konbu pan, using a slotted spoon or small sieve, and set them aside. Reduce the heat to low and add the rice and soy sauce to simmer for 10 minutes. Add the oysters and watercress and give it a gentle stir to mix. Serve with a pinch of grated ginger in the middle and sprinkle over the nori pieces.

**Cook's tip**

Serve with cauliflower miso gratin (see page 56), spicy stir-fried spinach with pancetta (page 58) or pot au feu of Chinese cabbage and bacon (page 60) for that really comforting effect.

# Crabmeat, spinach and shimeji ohitashi

There is no equivalent dish for *ohitashi* in Western cooking. The best way to describe it is a salad in broth. It is served warm in the winter and chilled in the summer. Eight portions of dashi stock to one portion of light soy sauce and a half portion of sake works well universally for the broth.

*200g baby spinach leaves*

*150g shimeji mushrooms*

*120g white crabmeat*

**for the ohitashi broth**

*400ml dashi stock (see pages 16–17)*

*50ml light soy sauce*

*25ml sake*

Blanch the spinach and drain well. Discard the base of the shimeji mushrooms and separate them. For the broth, mix the dashi, soy sauce and sake in a saucepan with the shimeji mushrooms and bring to the boil over a moderate heat. Reduce the heat to low and simmer for 2 minutes; turn the heat off and let it cool naturally with the shimeji mushrooms inside. When the broth has cooled to body temperature, add the crabmeat and spinach and gently stir to mix. Divide the mixture into four equal portions and serve warm.

**Cook's tip**

This recipe has three of my favourite winter ingredients, but you can experiment with your favourites. In the spring, try an ohitashi of asparagus with brown shrimps.

# Seared scallops with sweet-and-sour umeboshi sauce

Scallops are rich in protein, low in calories and contain vitamin B2, which metabolises sugar and fat, but the most notable nutrient is taurine, which prevents deterioration of eyesight and helps to restore tired optic nerves. They have the second highest zinc content among seafood after oysters. It is said that you use up more zinc if you are stressed. But I am sure this recipe will cause you no stress, as it is very simple with a delicious result.

12 large plump scallops,
   roe removed
½ teaspoon salt
1 tablespoon vegetable oil
1 bunch of watercress, trimmed

for the umeboshi sauce
50g granulated sugar
25ml water
2 tablespoons rice vinegar
1 tablespoon soy sauce
2 tablespoons umeboshi purée
   (pickled plums sold in tubes)

Slice the scallops horizontally into two, put them on a plate and sprinkle over the salt.

For the sauce, mix the sugar and the measured water in a small saucepan and let it come to the boil over a moderate heat. Add the vinegar and soy sauce, then reduce the heat to simmer for 5 minutes or until the sauce is reduced to a syrupy thickness. Take it off the heat, add the umeboshi purée and stir to dissolve. Set aside to cool.

Meanwhile, heat a griddle pan on a high heat. Brush the scallops with oil and sear for 1–2 minutes on each side.

Divide the watercress into four equal portions and arrange each portion on a serving plate. Put six scallop slices on to each serving and drizzle over the sauce to serve.

**Cook's tip**

You can buy umeboshi purée in the supermarket. It is umeboshi ready mashed and puréed.
Serve with warm bean sprout salad with crispy garlic (page 56) or green salad with Japanese salad dressing (see page 169).

# Clams in green vinegar sauce with somen noodles

This is a refreshing pasta sauce with clams and wakame seaweed. It is best served chilled with either fine somen noodles or soba noodles.

400g clams, scrubbed clean

200ml white wine

1/2 teaspoon salt

pinch of ground black pepper

200g dried somen noodles

1 large cucumber, peeled

1 tablespoon dried wakame
   seaweed, soaked in water

200g seedless green grapes,
   halved

few sprigs of flat-leaf parsley,
   roughly chopped (optional)

**for the vinegar sauce**

8 tablespoons rice vinegar

2 tablespoons water

2 tablespoons soy sauce

2 tablespoons sugar

Put the clams in a saucepan with the wine, salt and pepper and bring the liquid to the boil with its lid on. Steam the clams for 5 minutes or until all the shells have opened, shaking the saucepan continuously. Turn off the heat, remove the lid to let the clams cool enough to remove the shells and reserve the insides. Keep a few with their shells on for garnishing. Meanwhile, cook the somen noodles as described on the packet and leave them to drain in a colander. Grate the cucumber and squeeze it in your hands to rid it of excess water. Drain the wakame and roughly chop it. Put the clams, cucumber, green grapes and wakame pieces in a large bowl. Mix all the ingredients for the vinegar sauce, add to the clam and cucumber mixture and stir to incorporate them. Add the cooked noodles, divide them into four equal portions, garnish with the parsley and reserved clams and serve.

**Cook's tip**

If you are serving this dish chilled, refrigerate the cucumber mixture, covered with clingfilm, before adding the noodles. Do not refrigerate the noodles as it will make them stick together and turn into one big ball.

# Stir-fry of garlic squid with peppers

Many varieties of squid and cuttlefish are used in Japanese cooking. There is a preferred way of cooking each type but, in general, squid is prone to becoming hard and chewy when cooked so it is best to cook it very fast or not at all. Flash stir-frying is therefore an ideal way.

1 squid, weighing about 400g

1 green pepper

1 red pepper

1 tablespoon vegetable oil

1 garlic clove, peeled and cut into
matchstick-sized pieces

2 tablespoons sake

½ large red chilli, finely
chopped

1 teaspoon sesame oil

1 teaspoon salt

½ teaspoon rice vinegar

To prepare the squid, pull the tentacles off to remove the innards. Carefully remove the ink sac, which is attached above the eyes, and discard. Rub a clean damp cloth over the body to peel off the skin. Remove the cartridge from the body. Tear off the fins and, again with the damp cloth, remove the skin from the body part. Slice open the body and make criss-cross shallow insertions all over the body and fins to stop them curling when heated. Cut the body and fins into large postage-stamp-sized pieces. Cut the tentacles into 2–3 pieces.

Deseed the peppers and cut them into the same-sized pieces as the squid.

Heat a wok or a frying pan over a moderate/high heat and add the vegetable oil. Add the garlic pieces to infuse the oil and then quickly stir-fry the squid, adding the sake as it fries. Remove the garlic and squid with a large spoon and set aside.

Add the sesame oil, peppers and chilli and stir-fry for 2–3 minutes and then return the garlic and squid. Adjust the seasoning with salt and toss and stir. Take the wok off the heat, transfer the mixture on to a large serving dish and serve immediately.

**Cook's tip**

This is a very colourful main course dish, which can be served with new potatoes in spring and summer and roasted sweet potato with soy honey glaze (see page 54) or roast pumpkin and garlic mash (page 57) in colder months.

# Wakame and yam salad

Japanese people regard seaweeds as ocean vegetables and use over fifty varieties of them in various forms in their cuisine. Wakame is very healthy and contains no calories; it is full of calcium, iodine and other minerals. It prevents high blood pressure and hardening of the arteries, is rich in edible fibre, which prevents constipation, and its high iodine content helps the body's natural immunity. Outside Japan, wakame is available in either dried or salted form, which both need soaking in water before use.

20g dried wakame (seaweed)

150g yam, peeled and
    thinly sliced

5 tablespoons rice vinegar

1 pack of salad cress

handful of bonito flakes

3 tablespoons soy sauce

Soak the dried wakame in water for 10–15 minutes to soften and drain well. Soak the yam pieces in a bowl of water with the rice vinegar for 10–15 minutes and drain.

Put the wakame, yam, cress and bonito flakes in a salad bowl. Drizzle over the soy sauce and remaining rice vinegar, toss to dress and serve.

**Cook's tip**

This dish makes an excellent starter or accompanying side salad for any main course.

# poultry and eggs

**Cooking** with meat and poultry is not the first thing that comes to mind when you think of Japanese food. Although young Japanese people are eating more meat and poultry than their parents' or grandparents' generations, the amount is still small compared to the intake of other developed nations. There is no equivalent of roasting a large joint of meat or a whole chicken or turkey in Japanese cooking. Meat and poultry are butchered differently – generally they are sold in smaller, thinner cuts to suit Japanese ways of cooking and eating with chopsticks.

Chicken returned to the Japanese table in the mid-nineteenth century after a 1200-year absence and quickly gained popularity. In Japan today more chicken is eaten than any other meat. Chicken is popular for its gentler and leaner taste, its ability to partner other food and because it is less expensive than other meat, especially beef.

I am old enough to remember that in the early 60s there were specialist egg shops that sold nothing but eggs. A dozen eggs neatly laid out in a box of sawdust was a precious gift in those days. Eggs were an important source of scarce animal protein.

Today both chicken and eggs are the most intensively farmed foods and some of the cheapest food on the market. But at what cost, I wonder? I can't emphasise enough the importance of choosing the best-quality chickens and eggs to get the real taste and enjoyment of eating them. Otherwise you might as well take protein substitutes. In Japanese cuisine, you don't need large amounts of chicken or eggs, so you can afford to buy the best and ideally, support your local suppliers.

# Japanese-style chicken hamburger with grated daikon

There are many dishes that the Japanese have 'borrowed' from other cuisines and adapted to suit their food culture, and this is a good example. The good news is that this is one hamburger that doesn't leave you worrying about your waistline.

*100g firm cotton tofu, well drained (see page 110)*

*200g minced chicken*

*2 shallots, minced*

*1 garlic clove, peeled and minced*

*2 teaspoons peeled and grated fresh ginger*

*1 small free-range egg, lightly beaten*

*1 tablespoon cornflour*

*salt and black pepper*

*200g daikon (Japanese white radish), peeled and grated*

*juice of ½ lemon*

*2 tablespoons soy sauce*

*1 tablespoon vegetable oil*

In a large mixing bowl, mash the tofu with a fork and give the mash a final squeeze to rid it of any excess water.

Add the chicken, shallots, garlic, ginger, egg and cornflour and combine them well. Season with salt and pepper. Shape the mixture into four equal-sized patties of 2.5cm thickness. Put them on a plate lined with kitchen paper, cover with clingfilm and refrigerate for at least 2 hours to allow the flavours to develop.

Meanwhile, grate the Japanese white radish and combine with the lemon juice and soy sauce.

Heat the vegetable oil in a frying pan and cook the hamburgers for 5 minutes on one side, turn them over and cook the other side for a further 4 minutes. Serve with a generous dollop of grated radish.

**Cook's tip**

Try this recipe for your next barbecue served with a bowl of green salad and a noodle recipe like the soba noodle salad with smoked salmon, salmon roe and grated daikon (see page 143).

# Chicken yakitori

There is nothing so tempting as the aroma of grilled chicken wafting down the streets of Tokyo. Yakitori must be the nation's favourite bar snack. But you don't have to be over 18 years old (20 in Japan) to enjoy these mouth-watering mini kebabs. I marinate the chicken to minimise cooking time so that the meat remains succulent and the aroma of the soy-basting sauce is not burnt out.

*8 chicken mini fillets*

*for the marinade*

*4 tablespoons soy sauce*
*4 tablespoons sake*
*4 tablespoons mirin*
*1–2 tablespoons sugar*
*shichimi togarashi (Japanese*
*    seven-spice seasoning)*

*8 bamboo skewers, soaked*
*    in water*

Mix all the ingredients for the marinade in a bowl and add the chicken fillets to marinate for at least 2 hours.

Preheat the grill to the highest heat and line a baking tray with tinfoil to catch the drips of marinade (and make your washing up a lot easier). Put the bamboo skewers through the marinated fillets in a weaving motion. Paint the remaining marinade over the kebabs, place on the baking tray and grill for 5 minutes, then turn them over and grill for a further 3 minutes. Remove from the grill, sprinkle with the shichimi togarashi and serve 2 skewers to each diner, either hot or at room temperature.

**Cook's tip**

Serve at a summer barbecue with Japanese new potato salad (see page 44) and green salad. It also makes a great starter or a party finger food.

# Sake-steamed chicken parcels with pak choi

Steam-cooking is a gentle way of applying heat to an ingredient. It is a particularly suitable method of cooking delicate-flavoured ingredients such as chicken and vegetables. Be sure to get as good-quality chicken as possible because both the seasoning and cooking are simple, so the real flavour of the chicken comes through and there is no disguising it.

*4 chicken breast fillets,*
*  skin removed*
*½ teaspoon sea salt*
*4 tablespoons sake*
*1 teaspoon vegetable oil*
*1 pak choi, cut into*
*  bite-sized pieces*
*1 lime, quartered*

*4 sheets of A3-sized tinfoil*

Put the chicken in a bowl, rub with the salt and pour over the sake. Cover the bowl with clingfilm and refrigerate for at least 2 hours – preferably longer – to allow the sake to marinate and tenderise the chicken.

Lightly oil the central part of each tinfoil sheet. Place the chicken breasts and pak choi on them and pour over the sake marinade. Make a parcel by pulling in the four corners of each sheet, leaving generous headroom to allow the steam to circulate. Place the parcels in a large steamer and steam for 15–18 minutes over a moderate heat. If you are in any doubt about the cooking time, turn the heat off but leave the parcels in the steamer for a further 5 minutes before serving. Place the parcels on individual plates and serve each with a lime quarter. Let your guests open their own parcels.

**Cook's tip**

This makes an excellent dinner or party dish – everyone enjoys opening a culinary parcel.

# Soy-marinated roast chicken legs

Although you have to plan ahead and start the night before to let the full flavour develop and the chicken to tenderise, it is well worth the little extra effort. Try it once and I am sure you will agree.

4 chicken legs
1 tablespoon vegetable oil
1 teaspoon sesame oil

**for the marinade**
200ml soy sauce
10ml sake
10ml mirin
4 garlic cloves, peeled and grated
2 tablespoon sugar

Make 3–4 incisions on each chicken leg across the muscle tendon to help the marinade seep in better. Put the chicken in a bowl, mix all the marinade ingredients together and pour over the chicken. Marinate overnight in the fridge.

Preheat the oven to 190°C/375°F/gas mark 5. Take the chicken legs out of the marinade and pat them dry with kitchen paper. Mix the vegetable and sesame oils, brush the legs with them and roast for 25–30 minutes. Turn off the oven and leave the chicken inside until you are ready to serve. This way the chicken legs will be juicy and succulent.

**Cook's tip**
Why not serve with roasted vegetables of your choice and roasted sweet potato with soy honey glaze (see page 54)?

# Chicken teriyaki with ginger and vinegar

I am a self-confessed vinegar addict – I use it for cooking, soaking my hands, cleaning the kitchen and I even drink it as a nightcap. A dash of vinegar at the end of cooking highlights all the flavours of a dish – you don't need a single pinch of salt.

4 chicken thigh fillets, skin on
4 tablespoons cornflour
1 tablespoon vegetable oil
75ml teriyaki sauce (see page 167)
1 tablespoon peeled, grated
   fresh ginger
1 tablespoon rice vinegar

Place the chicken pieces skin-side down, make 3–4 incisions across the tendon of each one and dust with cornflour. Heat the oil in a frying pan and cook the chicken skin-side down over a moderate heat for 5 minutes or until the skin becomes golden and crisp. Turn over and place a lid on the pan to steam for 4 minutes. Remove the lid and add the teriyaki sauce and grated ginger. Shake the pan to coat the chicken evenly with the sauce. Add the rice vinegar and cook for a further 5 minutes, allowing the liquid to reduce slightly. Serve the chicken immediately with the cooking juices.

**Cook's tip**
Serve with any vegetables of your choice; I like steamed broccoli, cauliflower or green beans. Drizzle extra teriyaki sauce over the vegetables.

# Crispy duck breast with tangerine sauce on watercress

This is a Japanese version of the famous French dish *canard à l'orange*. The richness of the duck meat is well balanced with the bittersweet tangerine sauce and watercress. I am using just one duck breast for two servings because the breasts I buy from my village butcher are quite large and can easily supply two portions, but by all means adjust the amount to suit your appetite.

4 tangerines

2 duck breasts

2 tablespoons salt

vegetable oil

4 tablespoons sake

2 tablespoons soy sauce

100g watercress

Peel two of the tangerines and separate the segments. Remove the skin from each segment and set aside. Halve the other two tangerines, squeeze the juice out and reserve.

Lightly score through the skin and fat of the duck breasts with the tip of a very sharp knife. Take care not to cut into the flesh. Rub salt into the skin and incisions – this helps to release the fat and make the skin crisp.

Heat a heavy-based frying pan over a moderate heat and brush with oil. Place the breasts skin-side down and cook for 5–7 minutes to release the fat. Remove them from the pan. Discard the fat and return the pan to a high heat. Put the breasts skin-side up and cook for 2–3 minutes to seal. Turn it over and cook the other side for a further 5–6 minutes or until the skin becomes golden and crisp – depending on your preference. Remove the breasts to a warmed plate to rest for a few minutes before cutting it into manageable slices. Turn down the heat to low/moderate and add the sake to the meat juices in the pan. When the sauce is bubbling, add the tangerine juice and soy sauce and bring it back to the boil.

Meanwhile, divide the watercress into equal portions and arrange the duck slices on top. Scatter some tangerine segments around them, pour the sauce over them and serve.

**Cook's tip**

This is a full-flavoured rich main course dish so serve it with plain-cooked soba noodles, if desired. Use a fork to twist the noodles around to make small mounds.

# Japanese omelette with tomato and chives

A small amount of dashi stock makes an omelette light and succulent. For 1 egg, add 1 tablespoon of dashi, 1 teaspoon of sugar and 1 teaspoon of light soy sauce. Sugar brings out the egg's umami and gives a light gloss to the surface. It helps to have a square omelette pan but it is not essential – to prove my point, an ordinary round omelette pan is used here.

3 free-range organic eggs,
    lightly beaten
50ml dashi stock (see pages 16–17)
1 tablespoon sugar
1 teaspoon light soy sauce
1 ripe vine tomato, deseeded and
    finely chopped
6 chives, finely chopped
1 tablespoon vegetable oil

Mix all the ingredients, except the vegetable oil, in a mixing bowl. Soak some rolled-up kitchen paper with vegetable oil and have it ready. Heat an omelette pan over a moderate/high heat and brush with the oiled paper. Drop a teaspoon of the egg mixture into the pan to test the temperature – listen for a 'juwaaa' sound. Pour in about a quarter of the egg mixture and quickly spread to cover the whole of the pan.

When the egg mixture begins to bubble up, gather the egg towards you from the far side of the pan, using a pair of chopsticks or a spatula. Re-brush the uncovered area of the pan with the oiled paper. Push the omelette to the far side, re-brush the uncovered area and pour in another quarter of the egg mixture. Repeat the process of gathering, moving and re-oiling until all the egg mixture is used up.

Turn the omelette over to cook the underside. Transfer the omelette to a chopping board and place another straight-edged object against it to shape into a square. Cut into bite-sized slices and serve.

**Cook's tip**
This recipe makes a light starter or party finger food.

# Steamed savoury egg custard

This is one of my favourite dishes, not only for its delectable taste but also for the smooth, silky sensation on your tongue. In summer I suggest making it in advance and serving chilled.

2 free-range organic eggs,
  lightly beaten
300ml dashi stock
  (see page 16–17)
1 teaspoon light soy sauce
4 teaspoons salmon roe
4 medium prawns, cooked and
  shelled
2 teaspoons sake

In a mixing bowl, mix the beaten eggs with the dashi and soy sauce. Strain the mixture into another bowl through a fine sieve. Divide the mixture into four equal portions and pour into heat-resistant cups – attractive tea/coffee cups are ideal.

Place the cups in a steamer and put a tea towel under the lid to catch any condensation. The lid should be slightly skewed to let the steam escape. Steam for 2–4 minutes on a high heat, then reduce the heat to low and steam for a further 8 minutes.

Mix the salmon roe with the sake – sake separates the roe and takes away the fishiness. Remove the cups from the steamer, garnish with the prawns and roe and serve.

**Cook's tip**
Try serving this chilled in the summer.

# meat

**It is no** joke that eating beef was the most fashionable and politically correct thing to do in nineteenth-century Japan. In an attempt to modernise the country, the Japanese people aspired to and emulated every aspect of Western culture, including food. Emperor Meiji set a fine imperial example to the nation by eating beef for the first time in 1200 years at the New Year banquet in 1872 and replacing the palace menus with French cuisine. For a nation that had abstained from eating beef and poultry for such a long time, the Japanese quickly developed both a taste for and methods of rearing some of the finest-quality beef cattle in the world.

Kobe beef is internationally renowned for its quality and price. It is the brand name for a specially reared breed of Japanese beef cattle. In 1991 the Japanese domestic meat market was liberalised and cheap foreign imports flooded the country. Japanese beef farmers reorganised and decided to concentrate on high-value Japanese beef cattle rather than trying to compete against big and powerful producers like the USA and Australia. Names such as Kobe and Matsuzaka are among the most successful brands of beef.

Curiously, eating pork was never prohibited because pigs were kept for eating purposes only and never for agricultural labour nor for religious ceremonies. Lamb is a recent arrival at the Japanese table and probably will remain the least preferred type of meat because of its distinctive taste and smell.

Today the Japanese are eating eight times more meat than fifty years ago and now animal protein accounts for about a half of their total protein intake, though it is still small compared to that of Westerners. This is a huge increase and bound to affect the nation's state of health in generations to come.

Japanese ways of cooking with meat are distinctive; there is no tradition of roasting a large part of an animal. Meat is butchered and sold in smaller cuts and thin slices that are better suited to Japanese cooking and eating habits, which essentially involve surface heat and eating with chopsticks. Surprisingly small amounts of meat are required, since it is rarely cooked on its own. In Japan, while Buddhist principles, especially those of Zen Buddhism, are still revered and respected, vegetarianism is viewed with suspicion because it is not based on any religious belief and is seen as a fad without foundation.

The average Japanese person eats less than a quarter of the meat of his/her Western counterpart and probably feels quite happy about it. The little meat we eat, we certainly enjoy and make the most of. I have many friends who are so-called vegetarians and I love them all, though they do present me a challenge from time to time. I don't believe in cutting out anything from my diet – meat, fish, chocolate, bread, potatoes and so on – except wine during Lent, to remind me how to suffer.

# Japanese-style beef steak

I believe that the Japanese way of eating with chopsticks has many health benefits. It forces you to eat more slowly than if you were using a knife and fork or a spoon, so that you chew for a longer time and get more of the digestive juices flowing. This makes the food easier to digest and so is kinder to your digestive system. With chopsticks, you can pick up only a smaller amount at a time, so each mouthful is smaller. Slower eating and longer chewing also mean you eat less. In this recipe, fillet steaks are served in bite-sized pieces, designed to be eaten with chopsticks. The meat is cooked with a modest amount of ginger and garlic-infused oil, adding more flavour.

4 fillet steaks, each
   weighing 125–150g
salt and black pepper
4 tablespoons vegetable oil
100g fresh ginger, peeled
   and thinly sliced
2 garlic cloves, peeled
   and thinly sliced
8 shiitake mushrooms,
   stalks removed
1 leek, trimmed and
   sliced diagonally
4 tablespoons sake
4 tablespoons soy sauce
2 tablespoons mirin
12 sprigs of watercress

Take the beef out of the fridge and let it come to room temperature (as cold meat is tough and takes longer to cook). Season with salt and pepper and set aside. Heat a frying pan over a moderate heat and add the vegetable oil. Lower the heat and shallow-fry the ginger and garlic slices until they are golden and crisp. You may find it easier to do this if you tilt the frying pan to gather the oil in a small area of the pan. With a slotted spoon, take out the ginger and garlic slices and leave them to drain on a piece of kitchen paper. Empty the oil into a small bowl to reserve.

Increase the heat to moderate/high, return the frying pan to the heat, add 2 teaspoons of the infused oil and cook the shiitake mushrooms and leek. Remove the vegetables and keep them warm. Add another teaspoon of the oil to the pan and brown the meat on both sides. Put a lid on the frying pan to steam-cook for 1 minute. Take the meat out and keep it warm. Add the sake, soy sauce and mirin to the pan, let the sauce come to the boil and cook for 2 minutes to reduce.

Meanwhile, cut the meat into small bite-sized pieces and divide them between individual plates. Arrange the vegetables and watercress on the side, sprinkle the ginger and garlic slices on the meat, pour over the sauce and serve immediately.

**Cook's tip**
Serve with cooked green vegetables, such as broccoli, beans or spinach. Try spring beans with sesame miso (see page 45).

# Seared beef salad with watercress and grapefruit

This cooking method is called *tataki*, which literally means 'to hit' or 'to beat': you hit the meat with the palm of your hand to flatten and tenderise it. Traditionally the seared meat is plunged into iced water to stop further cooking and tighten it. But recently I have used rice vinegar instead – the purpose of searing is not to cook the meat through but to burn off the fat and seal in the taste, whereas plunging in ice water will congeal the fat you are trying to get rid of.

*200g rump or sirloin steak*

*1 teaspoon vegetable oil*

*salt and black pepper*

*2 tablespoons rice vinegar*

*1 grapefruit, segmented*

*100g watercress, trimmed*

*100g rocket*

*1 pack of salad cress*

**for the salad dressing**

*juice of 1 grapefruit*

*100g grated fresh ginger juice*
  *(see Cook's Tip on page 54)*

*1 teaspoon sugar*

*4 tablespoons soy sauce*

Take the meat out of the fridge and let it come to room temperature (as cold meat is tough and takes longer to cook). Brush the meat with the vegetable oil and rub with salt and pepper. Heat a griddle pan over a high heat and sear the meat on both sides. Place the meat on a chopping board and let it cool enough to handle. With a sharp knife, slice the meat into 5mm thick slices and pour over the rice vinegar. Separate each slice and give it a light but firm slap with the palm of your hand.

Remove the pellicle (thin skin) from each grapefruit segment. Put the watercress, rocket, salad cress and grapefruit in a salad bowl and arrange the meat on top. Mix the dressing ingredients, pour over the salad, toss and serve.

**Cook's tip**

This recipe can work very well as a main course for a smart dinner party. You can change the combination of salad to suit your preference.

# Japanese beefburger with shimeji mushrooms

In Japan, minced beef is rarely used on its own but combined with ground pork – the two varieties of meat complement each other in taste and nutrition and lighten the texture. In this recipe I also add finely chopped vegetables – a practice I began when my own children were very young and didn't always like eating certain vegetables, especially mushrooms. Now they are growing teenagers with the usual tastes for fast food, but I am happy and relieved that they still prefer this home-made beefburger.

**for the beefburgers**

200g lean minced beef

200g lean minced pork

1 medium onion, finely chopped

1/2 medium carrot, peeled
   and finely chopped

100g Portobello mushrooms,
   finely chopped

2 tablespoons cornflour

1 free-range egg, lightly beaten

1/2 teaspoon salt

generous amount of freshly
   ground black pepper

1 tablespoon vegetable oil

**for the mushroom sauce**

20g butter

2 garlic cloves, peeled and
   minced

100g shiitake mushrooms, stems
   discarded and thinly sliced

1 packet of shimeji mushrooms,
   weighing about 150g, separated

handful of flat-leaf parsley,
   finely chopped

3 tablespoons sake

1 tablespoon soy sauce

1 teaspoon miso paste

100ml crème fraîche

Put all the ingredients for the beefburgers, except the vegetable oil, in a large mixing bowl and use your clean hands to mix well. Divide the mixture into four equal portions and subdivide each quarter into three. I am allowing three mini burgers per person – small beefburgers cook faster and are easier to eat. Shape into twelve small even-sized oval patties of about 2.5cm thickness. Place them on a tray in a single layer, cover and set aside in a cooler part of your kitchen to allow the flavours to develop.

Heat a frying pan over a moderate heat and add the vegetable oil. Cook the mini burgers in small batches for 1–2 minutes or until browned. Reduce the heat and cook for a further 3 minutes on each side. Remove them from the pan and cover them to keep warm.

For the mushroom sauce, add the butter to the pan and fry the minced garlic. Add the mushrooms and cook for 3–4 minutes. Add the chopped parsley and season with sake, soy sauce and miso. Stir in the crème fraîche. Let the sauce come to the boil, then cook for 2 minutes.

Place three mini burgers on each plate, spoon on the mushroom sauce and serve immediately.

**Cook's tip**

The colour of miso paste is a good indication of its saltiness and texture – generally the darker-coloured miso is saltier and harder. Choosing a milk chocolate-coloured paste is a safe option.

# Simmered beef with celeriac

This recipe is an adaptation of a popular way of cooking meat with burdock; a long and thin aromatic root vegetable widely used in Japanese cooking. Burdock is, however, only available from Japanese grocery shops and does not keep fresh for a long time. So I came up with the idea of substituting the vegetable with celeriac and I think it works well.

400g celeriac, cut into slices like
  thick wood shavings
3 tablespoons rice vinegar
1 tablespoon vegetable oil
400g silverside or topside of
  beef, thinly sliced
1 medium onion, thinly sliced
100g fresh ginger, peeled and cut
  into matchstick-sized pieces
handful of coriander, roughly
  chopped

**for the cooking liquid**
100ml sake
100ml water
2 tablespoons sugar
100ml mirin
100ml soy sauce

Soak the celeriac in a bowl of cold water and the rice vinegar for 10 minutes – this refreshes the vegetable and keeps it crisp. Drain and transfer to a saucepan. Cover the celeriac with plenty of fresh cold water and bring to the boil over a high heat. Reduce the heat to low after it reaches boiling, cook for 5 minutes and drain.

Heat a wok or large frying pan over a moderate heat and add the vegetable oil. Add the beef and stir-fry for a few minutes or until it turns pale. Add all the ingredients for the cooking liquid in the order given and let it come to the boil. Add the celeriac, onion and ginger pieces. When the mixture returns to the boil again, reduce the heat to low and simmer for a further 10 minutes. Turn off the heat, add the coriander and stir. Transfer to a large serving dish and serve.

**Cook's tip**
Try serving this on top of plain boiled rice as a one-bowl lunch or supper.

# Pan-roasted loin of pork soused in soy

This is one of my favourite ways of cooking pork because it is fail-safe and has the added bonus of ending with a delicious, flavour-infused dressing.

300g loin of pork (fat trimmed)

1 teaspoon vegetable oil

**for the soy dressing**

200ml soy sauce

50ml sake

50ml mirin

1 garlic clove

3 tablespoons yuzu juice or
    lime juice

**for the salad**

200g watercress

1 medium cucumber, partly
    peeled and thinly sliced

1 pack of alfalfa sprouts

8 baby vine tomatoes, halved

Take the meat out of the fridge at least 30 minutes before you start cooking to let it come to room temperature (as cold meat is tough and takes longer to cook). Cut the loin lengthways into two. Heat a non-stick frying pan over a high heat and add the vegetable oil. Brown the meat all over and reduce the heat to moderate/low, cover the frying pan with a lid and cook for 15 minutes.

Meanwhile, mix all the ingredients for the soy dressing in a bowl. Plunge the meat into the dressing mixture and leave to souse for at least 3 hours, but preferably overnight, to allow the flavours to develop.

Cut the loin into thin slices, arrange these on top of the salad vegetables (or alternate with slices of cucumber as picture opposite), dress with the sousing liquid and serve.

**Cook's tip**

This recipe works very well as a one-dish lunch served with cooked soba noodles.

# Teriyaki pork steak

Succulent tender pork steak is perfectly matched with nutty sweet teriyaki sauce and a dash of rice vinegar highlights the taste and flavours.

4 pork steaks, each
   weighing 125g
4 tablespoons cornflour
1 tablespoon vegetable oil
4 tablespoons rice vinegar
handful of watercress

**for the teriyaki sauce**
4 tablespoons sake
4 tablespoons mirin
2 tablespoons sugar
4 tablespoons soy sauce
50g fresh ginger, peeled
   and grated

Take the meat out of the fridge at least 30 minutes before cooking (as cold meat is tough and takes longer to cook). Dust the steaks with the cornflour. Heat a frying pan over a moderate/low heat and add the vegetable oil. Sauté the steaks for 3 minutes on each side, then reduce the heat and cover the pan with a lid to steam-cook for a further 5 minutes.

Remove the lid and add all the ingredients for the teriyaki sauce. Shake the pan to coat the steaks evenly with the sauce and reduce it a little. Add the rice vinegar and stir the sauce. Remove the steaks and cut them into bite-sized pieces. Arrange the meat on individual plates, drizzle over the sauce and serve with a garnish of watercress.

**Cook's tip**
This teriyaki cooking sauce works equally well with lamb chops. Serve with cauliflower miso gratin (see page 56) or leek and carrot mini fritattas (page 60).

# Slow-cooked belly of pork

This is a real home-comfort slow food, taking two days to prepare what is often an underrated part of pork. The end result is simple but wholesome and tender. My grandmother used to say that you must be generous with your time because the pork will not be tender, but greasy, if you attempt to cook it in a hurry.

500g belly of pork

**for the aromatic marinade**
1 medium onion, halved
2 medium carrots, peeled
   and halved lengthways
2 celery sticks
50g fresh ginger, peeled and
   gently bruised
2–3 garlic cloves, peeled and
   gently bruised
1 teaspoon black peppercorns

**for the cooking liquid**
4 dried shiitake mushrooms,
   soaked in 100ml water
25g konbu (kelp seaweed)
175ml sake
100g light brown or golden
   granulated sugar
100ml soy sauce

Put the pork with all the ingredients for the aromatic marinade in a large heavy-based saucepan and add enough water to cover everything. Put the saucepan over a moderate heat and bring to the boil, skimming off any scum that floats to the surface. Reduce the heat to low and let it simmer for 2 hours.

Discard the vegetables and let the whole saucepan cool to room temperature. Refrigerate overnight. This is to solidify the fat and let the meat absorb all the flavour of the marinade.

Remove the solidified fat from the surface of the saucepan and reserve the soup. Cut the pork into 2.5cm cubes and place them in a large saucepan in a single layer. Cover the pork with a mixture consisting of two-thirds reserved soup and one third reserved water from the shiitake mushrooms. Place the konbu on top of the meat. Add the sake, sugar and softened shiitake mushrooms and bring to the boil over a low/moderate heat. Let it simmer for 30 minutes before adding the soy sauce and then slow-cook for a further 2 hours before serving.

**Cook's tip**
This makes a great winter warmer served with plenty of steamed vegetables and a dab of English mustard. It also goes particularly well with pot au feu of Chinese cabbage and bacon (see page 58).

# Gyoza – pork dumplings

Dumplings are known as *gyoza* in Japan and are very popular. They are a typical example of how Japanese cooks adapt and develop a classic Chinese dish into something of their own.

To make the dumpling mixture, discard the mushroom stems and finely chop the caps. Put all the ingredients for the dumplings in a bowl and mix well. Take one sheet of gyoza skin in your left palm and spoon 1 teaspoon of the dumpling mixture on to the centre of the skin. Wet the edge of the skin with a pastry brush. Fold over one half of the skin to enclose the filling, then make a few pleats. Put each dumpling on a tray lined with a sheet of baking paper. Repeat the process to use up all the mixture.

Heat a large frying pan over a moderate heat, add the vegetable oil, fill the pan with gyoza and cook until brown. Turn them over. When they are browned, reduce the heat, pour in a glass of cold water and immediately put a lid on to steam-cook the dumplings. Remove the lid to let the liquid evaporate and cook the dumplings for a further 3 minutes. Transfer the dumplings to a serving plate. Mix all the ingredients for the dipping sauce and serve with the gyoza.

## Cook's tip

The dumplings freeze very well and they can be cooked directly from frozen. Simply increase the cooking time and steam for a couple of minutes or so longer. The recipe works equally well with minced chicken or turkey instead of minced pork.
Try serving with warm bean sprout salad with crispy garlic (see page 57).

**for the dumpling mixture**

2 dried shiitake mushrooms, soaked in warm water for 10–15 minutes

100g pointed head or Savoy cabbage, finely chopped

100g ground pork

2 garlic cloves, peeled and finely minced

25g fresh ginger, peeled and finely minced

4 spring onions, finely chopped

1 tablespoon cornflour

1 teaspoon salt

2 teaspoons white pepper

150g fresh/frozen gyoza skins (48 sheets)

vegetable oil for pan-frying

**for the dipping sauce**

50ml soy sauce

50ml rice vinegar

2 teaspoons chilli sesame oil

# Pot-roasted rack of lamb with rice vinegar

Lamb is the most recent arrival at the Japanese table – in the early 1970s New Zealand mounted extensive marketing campaigns in Japan in an effort to find a new market for its lamb after Britain's entry to the then Common Market. It was a limited success. I love lamb and so does my family, but this is one area of cooking where I couldn't rely on my mother's or grandmothers' wisdom. So I created a new recipe with a Japanese twist and I hope you agree with me that it is rather yummy.

rack of lamb, providing
   2–3 lamb cutlets per person
2 tablespoons vegetable oil
1 large sprig of rosemary
100ml rice vinegar
50ml mirin
50ml sake
500g spinach
200g tinned cannellini or
   haricot beans
3 tablespoons soy sauce
2 tablespoons cornflour, mixed
   with 4 tablespoons water

Take the meat out of the fridge to let it come to room temperature (as cold meat is tough and takes longer to cook). Preheat the oven to 220°C/425°F/gas mark 7. Heat a very large, heavy-based flameproof casserole over a high heat and add the vegetable oil. Brown the meat on its fat side until the surface turns golden and crisp. Turn the meat to its bone side and place the rosemary underneath. Pour in the rice vinegar, mirin and sake and immediately put the lid on to bring the liquid to boil. Place the pan in the oven for 12–15 minutes, depending on how you like your lamb cooked.

Meanwhile, lightly steam the spinach and warm the beans.

Take the pan out of the oven and remove the meat, cover it and keep warm. Put the pan over a moderate heat to reduce the cooking liquid by a quarter, then add the soy sauce and the cornflour to thicken. Cut the rack into four portions and serve on a bed of spinach and beans with the sauce poured over it.

# tofu and beans

**Tofu** is one of the oldest processed foods of ancient China and has become a major source of vegetable protein throughout Southeast Asia. The Japanese people first learnt of tofu-making in the middle of the sixth century when Buddhism was introduced into Japan. As with many aspects of Chinese culture, the Japanese embraced tofu and refined it to suit the nation's cuisine.

Tofu is made of soya milk and comes in two varieties: the firm cotton variety and the soft silken type. It is rich in high-quality soya protein – 100g of tofu contains roughly half the amount of protein of chicken and a third of beef but is much easier to digest. Its oil content consists largely of linoleic acid, which helps to reduce cholesterol levels. Furthermore, tofu contains vitamins B1 and E, and zinc and kalium, which together help to prevent arteriosclerosis, high blood pressure, heart disease, osteoporosis and diabetes.

I am pleased to see tofu is becoming a healthy alternative to animal protein, not only among vegetarians but also among informed health-conscious people. Many organic food shops and Asian food stores sell fresh tofu. Tofu is best kept suspended in a bowl of clean water and refrigerated for up to 3 days. But despite all the good news, both tofu and beans suffer from an image of being rather bland and unsexy. Although both have a mild taste of their own, this makes them highly versatile and accommodating ingredients that can partner many. I hope to show that tofu is not just for Buddhist monks and vegetarians, but for everyone.

**Five ways of draining tofu**  Tofu is 90 per cent water. Although the water gives it its characteristic softness, some recipes call for drained tofu. Here are five ways of draining it.

**Natural way**  Put a block of tofu on a flat basket lined with a sheet of kitchen paper and leave it for 2–4 hours.

**Poaching method**  The length of poaching depends on the size of the tofu piece: from 2 minutes for small pieces to 15 minutes for a large whole piece.

**Microwave**  Although this is my least preferred method, it is handy if you are in hurry. Wrap the tofu in kitchen paper, place it at the centre of the turntable and microwave for 3–5 minutes at a medium setting.

**Squeezing method**  This is a quick and easy method if the shape of the tofu is unimportant. Wrap the tofu in a clean muslin cloth or tea towel and wring it hard to squeeze out the water.

**Pressing**  This is a good method if you need to retain the tofu's shape but are slightly short of time. Place the tofu on a chopping board, put another chopping board on top and add a weight – a tin of tomatoes is ideal. Depending on the weight, it takes 15–30 minutes to reduce the volume by a third.

# Seafood, tofu and glass noodle salad

This is a refreshing salad full of flavours and involves no cooking.

400g firm cotton tofu

50g vermicelli noodles

1/2 iceberg or Cos lettuce

200g ready-cooked mixed
 seafood

8 cherry tomatoes, halved

generous handful of fresh mint
 and coriander leaves,
 roughly chopped

**for the salad dressing**

4 tablespoons Thai fish sauce

4 tablespoons lime juice

1 1/2 tablespoons palm sugar
 or granulated sugar

4 tablespoons water

1 garlic clove, peeled and
 finely minced

1/2 large red chilli, finely minced

Break up the tofu into bite-sized chunks with your hands and leave to drain in a colander for at least 30 minutes.

Meanwhile, soften the noodles: put them in a heat-resistant bowl, cover with boiling water and leave for 10–15 minutes. Tear the lettuce into bite-sized pieces.

Drain the noodles and chop them into manageable-sized lengths with a pair of kitchen scissors. Mix all the ingredients for the dressing in a bowl and set aside.

In a large serving dish, toss all the salad ingredients together. Pour over the salad dressing, toss again and serve.

**Cook's tip**

Omit the seafood salad and replace the Thai fish sauce with soy sauce for a vegetarian version.

# Tofu cheese

Here are three easy ways to preserve tofu and make it more like cheese. Eat it on its own as a healthy snack, put it in salads or serve as tapas. See page 110 for notes on how to drain the tofu.

## Miso-flavoured tofu

200g medium-coloured miso of
  your choice
2 tablespoons mirin
200g firm cotton tofu,
  well drained

Mix the miso and mirin well. Cover the base of a glass container with a third of the miso mixture. Place the well-drained tofu in the container and cover it with the rest of the miso. Refrigerate for 3–4 days before eating. The miso mixture can be used once or twice more but reheat it to get rid of any excess water that has come out of the tofu.

## Red wine vinegar pickled tofu

200g soft silken tofu,
  well drained
1–2 garlic cloves, peeled and
  slightly crushed
4 tablespoons runny honey
200ml red wine vinegar

Cut the drained tofu into cubes to fit snugly in a glass preserving jar. Add the garlic. Mix the honey and vinegar well. Gently pour the vinegar mixture into the jar and set aside for 3–5 days to pickle at room temperature.

## Spicy chilli-flavoured tofu

200g firm cotton tofu,
  well drained
1–2 garlic cloves, peeled and
  slightly bruised
1–2 large chillies, deseeded and
  sliced lengthways
1 teaspoon salt
200ml extra virgin olive oil

Cut the drained tofu into bite-sized pieces. Put them in a glass preserving jar with all the other ingredients. Set aside for 3–5 days at room temperature.

# Four tofu dips

Tofu makes a perfect base for dips: it is easy to handle, its mild taste blends with any ingredient or seasoning and, above all, it is very healthy. Here are three quick and easy recipes for your party dips with a difference.

## Sesame and miso tofu dip

*200g tofu of your choice*

*4 tablespoons toasted sesame seeds*

*1 tablespoon sugar*

*2–3 tablespoons medium-coloured smooth miso paste*

*1–2 teaspoons soy sauce*

Drain the tofu with the squeezing method (see page 110). In a large mortar, grind the sesame seeds until smooth – the resulting paste should resemble smooth peanut butter (which is a perfect substitute for sesame paste). Add the drained tofu and the rest of the ingredients and continue to grind until the mixture is well incorporated and smooth. Adjust the seasoning with more soy sauce if necessary.

## Curry tofu dip

*200g firm cotton tofu*

*1 tablespoon curry paste*

*1 teaspoon soy sauce*

*1 teaspoon medium-coloured miso paste*

Drain the tofu with the squeezing method (see page 110). Put the tofu and other ingredients in a mortar and grind until the mixture is unified.

## Avocado and onion tofu dip

*200g soft silken tofu*

*1 ripe avocado, mashed*

*1 tablespoon lemon juice*

*1 shallot, finely minced*

*1 teaspoon Tabasco (optional)*

*salt and black pepper*

Drain the tofu with the squeezing method (see page 110). Put the tofu, avocado, lemon juice and shallot in a blender or food processor and blend until the mixture becomes smooth. Adjust the seasoning with Tabasco, salt and pepper.

# Tofu and avocado with wasabi soy dressing

Both silky tofu and buttery avocado have an affinity with a punchy wasabi soy dressing. You may keep the recipe as vegetarian or, if you wish, add a few slices of smoked salmon or crispy bacon bits. Either way, this is a quick and easy, healthy, fresh starter.

*400–600g soft silken tofu*
*1 ripe avocado*
*½ tablespoon lemon juice*
*1 ripe beef tomato, sliced*
*few basil leaves, torn or*
*    shredded*

**for the wasabi soy dressing**
*2 teaspoons wasabi powder,*
*    mixed with 2 teaspoons water*
*2 tablespoons soy sauce*
*½ teaspoon sugar or a drop*
*    of honey*
*3 tablespoons extra virgin*
*    olive oil*

Drain the tofu (see page 110) and refrigerate.

Meanwhile, put all the ingredients for the dressing in a small glass jar with a lid and shake vigorously to combine them.

Cut the chilled tofu into bite-sized pieces. Peel and slice the avocado, discarding the stone, and gently pour over the lemon juice to prevent discolouration.

Arrange the tofu, avocado and tomato on a large serving plate or individual plates. Shake the jar of dressing again and drizzle over the tofu and garnish with torn or shredded basil leaves and serve.

# Tofu, tomato and mushroom stew

This is a truly comforting dish – guaranteed to warm up the body and soul. Serve it with crusty bread to soak up all the juices.

400g soft silken tofu

1 tablespoon vegetable oil

1 onion, roughly sliced

2 celery sticks, destringed and
  roughly chopped

12 cherry tomatoes, halved

100g button mushrooms

3 tablespoons frozen peas

fresh flat-leaf parsley, chopped

**for the cooking liquid**

2 bay leaves

3 tablespoons white wine

100ml water

sprigs of oregano and thyme

salt and black pepper

To drain the tofu wrap it in kitchen paper and place 2–3 plates on top for 30 minutes. Chop the tofu into bite-sized pieces.

Mix together all the ingredients for the cooking liquid.

Heat the vegetable oil in a frying pan over a moderate heat. Add the onion and sweat for 5 minutes or until it is softened. Add the tofu cubes and brown them lightly. Add the rest of the vegetables and pour in the cooking liquid. Bring it to the boil, then reduce the heat to low and cook for a further 10 minutes before turning off the heat. Adjust the seasoning with salt and pepper. Garnish with the parsley and serve.

**Cook's tip**

Although I call this a stew, it is in fact a very quick dish to prepare. But if you prefer to cook it in the oven, omit all the pre-cooking, put everything in a buttered ovenproof dish and place it in the oven for 20 minutes. I also find a sprinkle of nutmeg really brings out the flavour.

# Tofu steak with garlic and mushrooms

Who said tofu is for genteel vegetarians? Tofu has about a third of the amount of protein in beef without the worries of high cholesterol. This is a substantial main-course dish packed with taste and health that could easily out-flavour a beef steak.

Drain the tofu (see page 110). It is a matter of personal choice, but don't overdo as it will leave you with rather solid steaks.

Heat the vegetable oil in a frying pan and sauté the garlic slices until they become crisp and the oil is infused. Add the mushrooms and cook until they become soft. Season with soy sauce and adjust the taste with salt and pepper.

Spoon the mushrooms and their cooking juices out and keep them warm. Add more oil if necessary and cook the drained tofu steaks on one side for 5–7 minutes or until they turn crispy golden brown. Cook on the other side. Put the tofu on warmed plates and spoon over the mushrooms and crispy garlic slices. Garnish with the chopped spring onions and serve immediately.

**Cook's tip**

Why not serve this with purple-sprouting broccoli with mustard soy dressing (see page 36), grilled asparagus in dashi (page 38), or string beans with sesame miso dressing (page 45)?

*4 firm cotton tofu blocks, each*
  *weighing 200g*
*1 tablespoon vegetable oil*
*2 garlic cloves, peeled and*
  *thinly sliced*
*60g shimeji mushrooms,*
  *separated*
*4 shiitake mushrooms, stalks*
  *discarded and caps sliced*
*2 tablespoons soy sauce*
*salt and black pepper*
*2 spring onions, finely chopped*

# Tofu sashimi with spicy hot oil

This recipe is inspired by both Chinese and Vietnamese cuisine. The only cooking required is to make the garlic- and chilli-infused oil.

400g soft silken tofu, drained
  (see page 110) and chilled
2 tablespoons rice grains
2 tablespoons soy sauce

**for the spicy oil**
1 large red chilli
4 tablespoons grapeseed oil or
  sunflower oil
1 teaspoon sesame oil
2 garlic cloves, peeled and
  slightly crushed

Cut the drained tofu into bite-sized pieces and arrange them on individual serving plates. Refrigerate.

To dry-toast the rice grains, heat the rice in a small non-stick frying pan over a high heat, constantly shaking the pan. Grind the toasted rice with a pestle and mortar.

For the spicy oil, cut 2–3 incisions lengthways on the chilli. In a small saucepan, heat the oil, garlic and chilli over a very gentle heat. Discard the chilli and garlic when they turn light brown. Turn the heat up high. Take the plates of tofu out of the fridge, pour over the soy sauce and sprinkle over the ground rice. When the oil is almost smoking, pour it over the tofu and serve immediately.

# Warm tofu and steamed vegetable salad with plum dressing

You can make this salad as substantial as you wish by adding steamed vegetables of your choice. You may also add shredded steamed chicken breast.

400g soft silken tofu, drained

400g spinach

200g bean sprouts, roots
  trimmed

1 medium carrot, peeled
  and cut into matchstick-
  sized pieces

8 fresh shiitake mushrooms,
  sliced

2 tablespoons vegetable oil

1 teaspoon sesame oil

**for the umeboshi dressing**

4 umeboshi (pickled plums),
  finely mashed

1 garlic clove, peeled and grated

1 tablespoon sugar

1/2 teaspoon salt

6 tablespoons rice vinegar

1 tablespoon soy sauce

Wrap the tofu with kitchen paper and leave to drain for 30 minutes. Bring a saucepan of water to the boil and add the spinach, then immediately turn off the heat and drain. Squeeze the excess water out of the spinach. Steam the rest of the vegetables and cover them to keep warm.

Mix all the ingredients for the umeboshi dressing and set aside.

Cut the drained tofu into 1.5cm cubes. Arrange the vegetables and tofu in a large warm serving dish. Put the vegetable oil and sesame oil in a metal cooking spoon and heat until the oil mixture is almost smoking hot. Pour it over the salad and add the dressing. Toss and serve immediately.

# Japanese bean ratatouille

This is based on an old bean dish called *gomokumame* – five kinds of beans – which has no fixed ingredient but is just a frugal way of using up vegetable off-cuts with soya beans. Konbu and dried shiitake mushrooms with the soy-based cooking liquid give a homely, comforting taste to the dish. I use tinned mixed beans, which are available from supermarkets for convenience.

Dried beans of any variety need an overnight soaking in water and long cooking to soften them. Soak the beans in a large saucepan with four times their volume of water overnight. Rinse the beans and change the water. Cover the beans with enough water and bring to the boil over a high heat, reduce the heat to low/moderate once it reaches the boil and continue to simmer for 45-60 minutes.

*1 postcard-sized piece of dried*
*konbu (kelp seaweed)*
*2–3 dried shiitake mushrooms*
*200g mixed beans, drained*
*1 small carrot, peeled and cut*
*into small dice*
*2 tablespoons sugar*
*½ teaspoon salt*
*2 tablespoons soy sauce*

With a pair of kitchen scissors, cut the konbu into small postage-stamp-sized pieces and leave them in enough warm water to soften. Reserve the liquid.

Soften the shiitake mushrooms in enough warm water to cover. Drain, reserving the liquid, and chop the caps into similar-sized pieces to the konbu.

Put the drained beans, konbu, mushrooms and diced carrot in a saucepan with the reserved liquids. Add the sugar and bring to the boil over a moderate heat. Reduce the heat to low once the mixture reaches boiling point and continue to simmer for a further 15–20 minutes or until the liquid is almost evaporated. Turn off the heat and adjust the seasoning with salt and soy sauce before serving.

**Cook's tip**
The bean ratatouille will keep for 2–3 days at room temperature. You can serve it as a small side dish or with salad leaves.

# Soya beans with bonito flakes

Soya beans are the favourite and the most important beans for Japanese cuisine. There are so many ingredients and seasonings that are made of them – miso paste, soy sauce and tofu, to name but a few.

½ tablespoon vegetable oil

150g soya beans, soaked
  and drained (see page 122)

1 tablespoon sake

1 tablespoon mirin

1 tablespoon soy sauce

½ teaspoon chilli flakes

5g bonito flakes

Heat a frying pan over a low heat and add the vegetable oil. Add the softened beans and sauté for a few minutes. Add the sake, mirin and soy sauce and let the cooking liquid reduce by half. Sprinkle over the chilli flakes and add the bonito flakes. Toss the beans to mix and serve either hot or at room temperature.

# Broad bean frittata

I invented this recipe when my children complained that they had simply had enough of our home-grown broad beans. This makes a tasty one-plate lunch or starter served with a drizzle of teriyaki sauce (see page 171).

200g fresh broad beans, podded

100g cooked prawns

1 free-range egg, lightly beaten

2 spring onions, finely chopped

2 tablespoons rice flour or
  cornflour

1 tablespoon light soy sauce

1 teaspoon peeled, grated
  fresh ginger

1 tablespoon vegetable oil

Cook the broad beans in a saucepan of boiling water for 10–15 minutes or until they are soft. You should be able to squash a bean between your thumb and index finger. Drain, rinse under cold running water and remove the skins.

Put the beans and prawns in a blender or food processor and process very briefly – some of the beans and prawns should be identifiable in shapes. Put the mixture in a bowl, add the rest of the ingredients, except the vegetable oil, and mix well.

Heat the oil in a frying pan and pour in the mixture. Even it out with a spatula to make a flat pancake. Cook on one side for 6–8 minutes over a moderate heat. Turn it over to cook the other side for a further 5 minutes. Serve immediately.

# rice and sushi

**A third** of the world's population depends on rice for its staple diet. Indeed rice is the staple food of Japan, but for the Japanese the real meaning of this humble grain goes far beyond the boundaries of food. Rice and Japanese history, politics, economy, religion, culture and in fact almost every aspect of the country and its nation's life are inextricably tied together. The labour-intensive and high-maintenance demands of rice cultivation are said to have contributed to forming the industrious and group-cohesive characteristics of the Japanese people. Rice is the soul of Japan and those who understand it hold the key to a real understanding of the country and Japanese cuisine.

Rice plays the central role in Japanese cooking. Whether it is early spring and the very first succulent bamboo shoots are available from Kyoto, or the freshest wild sea bream sashimi from the Shimonoseki Straits or a thick juicy Kobe beef steak, a humble bowl of cooked rice is the main dish and everything else is an accompanying side show. In the Japanese language, the word for cooked rice, *gohan*, is the same as the word for a meal. Millions of Japanese mothers and wives call out, '*Gohan desuyo*' when a meal is ready because rice and a meal are synonymous.

Nutritionally, rice comprises 75 per cent carbohydrate and 8 per cent protein, which is the highest protein content of all grains. However, much of the goodness such as edible fibre, vitamins and minerals are lost in the polishing. In the past, polished white rice was considered the best and was what all Japanese people aspired to eat. In my grandmothers' era the loss of those nutrients in rice was easily made up by other food, which was not as highly processed as the food we eat today. While unpolished brown rice is harder to digest, it is unquestionably healthier than white rice; it has four times more edible fibre, vitamins B1 and E, and twice as much vitamin B2, fat, iron and phosphorus than polished white rice. After the economic boom of the 1980s followed by over a decade of recession, Japanese people seem to have rediscovered the wisdom of simpler traditional ways of eating that are kinder and more suited to their bodies and souls.

Today Japanese people are eating about half the amount of rice that they used to forty years ago. In 2000, the average annual rice consumption *per capita* fell below 65kg after peaking at 118.3kg in 1962. The irony is that brown rice has become the preferred choice of informed and health-conscious Japanese people, rather than polished white rice, which used to be revered as a food for the rich and powerful.

My grandmothers believed in the nourishing and healing power of rice, especially when it was cooked as a *congee* – soupy rice. If I sneezed more than three times, I was sure to be given a bowl of steaming creamy miso, white spring onion and ginger congee. When I had a bad tummy, it was a bowl of warm silky white rice congee with a spoonful of pickled plums to make me better. Congees are the ultimate comfort food – versatile and easy to digest as well as being simple to make, like a risotto without the constant stirring.

# Asparagus and broad bean domburi

*Domburi*, which translates as 'on rice', is the Japanese equivalent of baked beans on toast. It is a quick and easy, satisfying one-bowl snack – almost anything can be turned into a tasty topping sauce served on rice. In this recipe, two spring vegetables are used together.

*40 broad beans*

*110g frozen cooked shrimps or small prawns*

*2 asparagus spears*

*200ml water*

*2 teaspoons vegetable oil*

*1 tablespoon light soy sauce*

*½ teaspoon rice vinegar*

*1 tablespoon cornflour, mixed with 2 tablespoons water*

*salt and black pepper*

*400g cooked rice, (Japanese-style short-grain or brown) kept warm*

Pod the broad beans to yield 40 individual beans and boil them for 3 minutes, drain and let them cool before removing the skin from each bean. I know this is fiddly but the end result makes such a difference in taste, colour and texture; it is well worth the extra effort.

Meanwhile put the frozen shrimps in the measured water to defrost and soak. Discard the stringy lower ends of the asparagus spears and slice the rest diagonally.

Heat a wok or frying pan over a moderate heat and add the oil. Stir-fry both the broad beans and asparagus for 2–3 minutes, then add the prawns and the water. Let the mixture come to the boil and reduce the heat. Season with the soy sauce and vinegar and add the cornflour mixture to thicken the sauce. Adjust the taste with salt and pepper. Divide the cooked rice among individual bowls, put the asparagus and bean mixture on top and serve.

**Cook's tip**
The recipe works equally well if you use white crabmeat or any white fish flakes instead of shrimps.

# My version of New Year herbal congee

The seventh of January is known as the day of *nanakusa* (seven herbs) and it is the tradition on that day in Japan to prepare and eat seven-herb congee to pray for the good health of the family for the rest of the year. When I was a little girl, I followed my grandmother to nearby fields to forage for those seven wild herbs, such as wild celery, shepherd's purse, wild chrysanthemum and chickweed, which at that time I thought were more like weeds.

The tradition of preparing the seven-herb congee on the seventh day of January lives on in Japan, perhaps because the herbs (specially grown for the day) can now be bought from supermarkets. Scepticism aside, it does make good sense to treat your body gently with an easily digestible congee after the Christmas and New Year festive indulgence. I have created my own version of the seven-herb congee with more familiar vegetables and herbs, but have kept the integrity of the original recipe.

*200g Japanese-style brown rice, rinsed*

*4 dried shiitake mushrooms*

*1 litre dashi stock (see pages 16–17) or water*

*1 medium leek, trimmed and thinly sliced*

*50g purple-sprouting broccoli, roughly chopped*

*25g flat-leaf parsley, finely chopped*

*50g spinach, roughly chopped*

*50g rocket leaves, roughly chopped*

*25g coriander leaves, finely chopped*

*1 heaped tablespoon light-coloured miso paste*

*2 tablespoons light soy sauce*

*salt*

*1 tablespoon rice vinegar*

*1 tablespoon toasted sesame seeds*

Rinse the rice until the water runs clear and set it aside in a sieve or colander for at least 1 hour (but preferably 2 hours) before cooking. In a large heavy-based saucepan, put the shiitake mushrooms, stock or water and the rice, which has plumped up after being rested and having absorbed the moisture around it. With the lid on, bring the liquid to the boil over a moderate heat and reduce the heat to low once it begins to boil; stir occasionally.

Fish out the shiitake mushrooms and let them cool before discarding the stems. Thinly slice the caps and put them back into the rice. Add the leek and purple-sprouting broccoli, stir and allow to come back to the boil before adding the parsley, spinach, rocket and coriander.

Gently stir and bring back to the boil again. Add the miso paste (the taste of the miso should not be prominent but it gives a subtle depth to the broth) and soy sauce. Adjust the seasoning with salt and turn off the heat. Pour in the rice vinegar and stir. Sprinkle over the sesame seeds and serve immediately.

# Spicy garlic and chive fried rice

In a Japanese household, there is always some leftover cooked rice and there are numerous ways of making it into tasty dishes. This recipe is one of my summer staples, the other being simple cold noodles. It is very easy and quick to make but, above all, it has a truly appetising scent and flavour – guaranteed to pick you up when you are feeling a little under the weather in the summer heat.

2 tablespoons vegetable oil

1 teaspoon sesame oil

50g garlic, peeled and minced

400g cold cooked rice (Japanese-
   style short-grain or brown)

1 large red chilli, deseeded and
   finely chopped

25g chives, finely chopped

1 heaped teaspoon curry powder

2 tablespoons soy sauce

salt and black pepper

25g coriander leaves,
   roughly chopped

Put a wok or large non-stick frying pan over a high heat and add the vegetable oil. Reduce the heat to moderate and add the sesame oil and minced garlic to cook until the oil has become infused and the garlic is golden. Add the rice and, with a spatula, make cut-and-turn motions to coat the rice with the oil and heat for 3 minutes.

Add the chopped chilli and chives and mix, using the cut-and-turn motion. Sprinkle over the curry powder. Drizzle the soy sauce around the edge of the wok and stir. Adjust the taste with salt and pepper and turn the heat off. Garnish with the chopped coriander leaves and serve immediately.

# Leek, hijiki and tofu congee

This is a truly nourishing, tasty and above all comforting dish of a soupy rice with a miso flavour. Although it is a vegetarian recipe, both tofu and miso supply masses of protein, while hijiki (seaweed) is packed with minerals, not to mention edible fibre and leeks are known to ward off colds. Altogether this is a perfectly balanced winter dish to keep your body and soul warm and healthy.

200g firm cotton tofu, drained
  (see page 110)
4 dried shiitake mushrooms
1 postcard-sized piece of konbu
  (kelp seaweed)
1 litre water
2 medium leeks, trimmed
  and thinly sliced diagonally
4 tablespoons hijiki (seaweed)
400g cooked rice (Japanese-style
  short-grain or brown)
4 tablespoons soy sauce
100g medium-coloured miso
  paste of your choice

Drain the tofu as described on page 110.

Meanwhile, put the shiitake mushrooms, konbu and water in a heavy saucepan. Put the saucepan over a low heat and bring to the boil. Add the sliced leeks, hijiki and cooked rice and continue to simmer for 15 minutes, stirring occasionally, to thicken.

Cut the drained tofu into bite-sized pieces and add them to the rice mixture. Return to the boil and season with the soy sauce and miso paste. Dissolve the miso paste gradually by adding it with a small amount of liquid or by putting the paste in a sieve and mixing it into the liquid. Bring back to the boil, turn off the heat and serve immediately.

# Shimeji mushroom and chicken rice

This is an autumn comfort dish packed with flavour. By adjusting the amount of liquid, you can make it more like soupy risotto or fluffy pilaff, depending on your mood. The recipe is to make the latter.

200g Japanese-style short-
  grain rice
4 mini chicken breast fillets,
  sliced diagonally
1 tablespoon sake
1 tablespoon soy sauce
1 packet of shimeji mushrooms
  (weighing about 150g)
few sprigs of coriander,
  roughly chopped
1 lime, cut into 8 wedges

for the cooking liquid
225ml dashi stock
  (see pages 16–17)
2 tablespoons sake
2 tablespoons soy sauce
1 tablespoon mirin

Put the rice in a sieve resting in a bowl, pour over just enough water to cover and give it three or four firm stirs with your hand. Change the water and do the same again – you will probably have to repeat this stir-and-rinse process a further two or three times before the water becomes clear. Drain the rice and set it aside for at least 30 minutes, but preferably 1 hour.

Meanwhile, put the chicken in a bowl with the sake and soy sauce and set aside until the rice is ready to cook. Cut off the base of the shimeji mushrooms where they are joined and separate them.

Put the rice in a heavy-based saucepan with a tight-fitting lid, add the ingredients for the cooking liquid and stir to mix. Bring to the boil over a moderate heat. Let it boil for 3 minutes and add the chicken and mushrooms, lower the heat and allow to steam-cook with the lid on for 15 minutes. Turn off the heat and let it steam for a further 10 minutes before lifting the lid to stir. Garnish with the chopped coriander and serve with lime wedges.

# Sushi

A high-ranking Japanese diplomat once told me that the humble piece of sushi has probably been more successful in raising Japan's profile on the international stage than all his official efforts. I thought that he was a little too hard on himself but there is a grain of truth in it. Sushi has put Japan on the world culinary map. When I first came to England in the early 1970s, there was only a handful of Japanese restaurants in London. Now there are over one hundred in the capital alone and more than half of them serve sushi regularly. Never in my wildest dreams did I think that thirty years later I would see sushi lunch boxes on sale next to sandwiches in supermarkets. Sushi is a perfect portable meal – a fresh, healthy and good-looking food that is easy to eat anywhere at any time. But sushi is not all about little rice nuggets and slices of raw fish; *nigiri zushi*, the hand-formed sushi, is only one type. It is a relative newcomer in the context of the lengthy evolution of sushi, which began as a way of preserving fish that took as long as a year to make. Sushi has evolved from an ancient slow food to a contemporary fast food with widespread international recognition.

Sushi comes in a wide variety of styles and shapes; each family has its own favourite repertoire and there are countless regional specialities found across Japan. *Chirashi zushi*, or scattered sushi, is a generic term for free-form rice salad that is the easiest to make, highly versatile and very homely. A big dish of scattered sushi always graces the table at family gatherings. The choice of toppings is infinite but I always try to remember the simple principle of choosing seasonal ingredients that work well together in taste, texture and appearance.

It is impossible to cover the whole spectrum of sushi in one small section of a book when the subject deserves an entire book of its own. I have put together delicious, easy-to-prepare scattered sushi recipes for this section.

# How to prepare sushi rice

Good sushi begins with good rice. Try to choose good-quality Japanese-style short-grain rice, which you can buy from large supermarkets and Asian stores. The rice is first cooked and seasoned with a sushi vinegar mixture of rice vinegar, salt and sugar. Once prepared, sushi rice needs to be covered with a clean damp cloth until needed and should be used within the same day. There is no need to refrigerate it as the vinegar has an anti-bacterial preservative quality; and refrigeration spoils the delicate flavour and hardens the rice. In Japan, every sushi shop has its own sushi vinegar recipe – the general rule is that the stronger the filling or topping served with it, the saltier and less sweet the vinegar mixture. The amount given below is a basic guide.

300g Japanese-style short-
grain rice
1 postcard-sized piece of konbu
(dried kelp seaweed)
330ml water

**for the sushi vinegar mixture**
6 tablespoons rice vinegar
2 tablespoons sugar
1 teaspoon salt

Put the rice in a sieve and submerge in a large bowl of water. With your hand, keep circling the rice to wash it, then discard the milky water. Keep washing the rice and changing the water until it runs clear. After the final draining, set the rice aside for at least 30 minutes to absorb the moisture clinging to the grains.

Make a few incisions in the konbu to help release its flavour as it cooks. Put the rice, measured water and konbu in a heavy-based saucepan with a tight-fitting lid. Bring to the boil over a low/moderate heat. Resist the temptation to lift the lid to take a look while it is cooking but learn to listen for the bubbling sound of boiling. Turn up the heat and cook for a further 3–5 minutes, then turn off the heat and leave the rice to steam for 10–15 minutes.

Put the vinegar, sugar and salt in a non-metallic bowl and stir to dissolve the sugar and salt. Transfer the cooked rice into a moistened (to stop the rice sticking), shallow, flat-based basin (an oil-free, wooden salad bowl is ideal). Sprinkle a small amount of the sushi vinegar mixture over a spatula into the rice. At the same time, have someone standing by to fan the rice. With a cut-and-turn motion, coat the grains of rice with the vinegar mixture and separate them. Continue to sprinkle the vinegar to mix into the rice until it begins to look glossy and has cooled to room temperature. Cover the rice with a clean damp cloth and set aside until needed.

# Broccoli and scrambled egg scattered sushi

Try to use tenderstem or purple-sprouting broccoli, which I love for their taste and texture.

*25g butter*

*2 free-range eggs, lightly beaten*

*1 tablespoon mirin*

*pinch of salt*

*200g broccoli (preferably tenderstem or purple-sprouting), trimmed*

*1 tablespoon rice vinegar*

*350g prepared sushi rice (see page 133)*

*1 tablespoon sesame seeds*

*2 tablespoons shredded nori*

Melt the butter in a non-stick frying pan over a moderate heat. Pour in the beaten eggs with the mirin and use two pairs of chopsticks to scramble the egg mixture into tiny fluffs. When you think you have scrambled enough, turn off the heat and let the egg cool in the frying pan.

Meanwhile, chop the broccoli diagonally into small pieces and steam. Pour in the rice vinegar into a large, non-metallic bowl and swirl it around to coat the inside – this will stop the rice sticking to the bowl. Add the prepared sushi rice and the steamed broccoli pieces and mix well. Transfer the sushi mixture on to a large serving dish, sprinkle the scrambled eggs and the sesame seeds over the top, garnish with the shredded nori and serve.

**Cook's tip**

Try this recipe with steamed asparagus in the late spring. I often add salmon flakes (see page 73) to make a one-course meal.

# Smoked salmon, salmon roe and caper sushi

I had to invent this recipe when I was warned at the eleventh hour that one of my dinner-party guests 'really does not care for raw fish but loves sushi'.

2 tablespoons rice vinegar

350g prepared sushi rice
 (see page 133)

juice of 1 lime

250g smoked salmon offcuts

3 tablespoons capers, drained

1 tablespoon sake

1 jar of salmon roe

Moisten the inside of a large mixing bowl with the rice vinegar to stop the rice sticking. Put in the prepared sushi rice and pour over the lime juice to help loosen the rice. Add the smoked salmon bits and capers and mix with a flat spatula using a cut-and-turn motion. Add the sake to the salmon roe – this helps to take away its fishy smell and makes the roe less sticky. Transfer the sushi mixture on to a large serving platter, scatter the salmon roe on top and serve.

**Cook's tip**
If you find it difficult to get salmon roe (normally sold in small glass jars), try finely scrambled eggs instead.

# Marinated tuna, avocado and white onion sushi

This recipe shows a great partnership between Japanese and Western ingredients.

200g sashimi-quality tuna

1 small white onion

1 ripe avocado

1 tablespoon rice vinegar

350g prepared sushi rice
 (see page 133)

2 tablespoons wasabi powder,
 mixed with 2 tablespoons water

1 sheet of dried nori, finely shredded

**for the marinade**

3 tablespoons soy sauce

1 tablespoon mirin

2 teaspoons wasabi powder,
 mixed with 4 tablespoons water

3 tablespoons toasted sesame seeds

Slice the tuna into 5mm-thick pieces. Mix all the marinade ingredients together and marinate the tuna for 15–20 minutes.

Meanwhile, finely slice the white onion and put in a bowl of ice-cold water – soaking gets rid of the onion's smell and freshens it up. Peel the avocado, slice it into similar-sized pieces as the tuna and sprinkle with the rice vinegar to prevent discolouring.

Divide the prepared sushi rice into four and put into individual serving dishes. Place the avocado pieces over the sushi rice and arrange the marinated tuna on top. Drain the onion slices and divide into four portions to scatter on top of the tuna. Place a small mound of wasabi paste on the centre, garnish with shredded nori and serve.

# Prawn, pomegranate and green chilli sushi

The pomegranate originates in the Middle East and is widespread throughout Asia. They were brought to Japan from China in the twelfth century; the flowers were used for ornamental and the fruits for medicinal purposes. There are many references to them in mediaeval Japanese paintings and literature.

2 ripe pomegranates

4 tablespoons pomegranate juice

350g prepared sushi rice (see page 133)

200g cooked prawns

1–2 large green chillies, finely chopped

few sprigs of coriander and mint leaves

Halve the pomegranates horizontally, separate the individual fruitlets from the rind and reserve. Moisten the inside of a large mixing bowl with 2 tablespoons of the pomegranate juice to stop the rice sticking. Add the prepared sushi rice, sprinkle over the remainder of the pomegranate juice to separate the rice and mix. Add the cooked prawns, chopped chillies and reserved pomegranate and mix with a flat spatula in a cut-and-turn motion. Transfer the sushi mixture into either a large serving dish or individual dishes. Garnish with the coriander and mint leaves and serve.

**Cook's tip**

This recipe works equally well with white crabmeat instead of prawns.

# Chicken teriyaki and edamame sushi salad

Here is a recipe for meat-eating sushi lovers. An unusual combination of chicken and sushi rice works well, and including edamame is an additional bonus.

300g chicken thigh fillets,
   without skin
2 tablespoons cornflour
1 tablespoon vegetable oil
100ml teriyaki sauce
   (see page 167)
100g frozen edamame
a little rice vinegar (optional)
350g prepared sushi rice
   (see page 133)
1 sheet of dried nori, torn into
   small pieces

Cut the chicken thighs into small bite-sized pieces and dust them with the cornflour. Heat a non-stick frying pan over a moderate heat and add the vegetable oil. Sauté the chicken for 5 minutes or until golden. Add the teriyaki sauce and bring to the boil, then reduce the heat to low to simmer until the liquid has almost disappeared.

Meanwhile, either steam or boil the edamame for about 3 minutes. Depod them, if needed, and set them aside.

Moisten the inside of a large mixing bowl with either water or, better still, rice vinegar to stop the rice sticking. Add the prepared sushi rice and the chicken and mix with a flat spatula in a cut-and-turn motion. Transfer the sushi mixture on to a large serving dish, scatter the edamame on top, garnish with the nori pieces and serve.

**Cook's tip**
If you find it difficult to get edamame try using frozen baby broad beans instead. You can prepare this in advance – up to 3 hours beforehand – but do not garnish with the nori until just before serving or it will become limp.

# noodles

**Like so many** things, the technique of noodle-making originally came to Japan from China over a thousand years ago. Noodles have become native in Japan and have developed their own national identity. Japanese noodles are broadly divided into two groups by their ingredients – wheat and buckwheat. Wheat-based udon and somen noodles are more popular in the warmer and more fertile south-western part of Japan, while soba noodles, made of buckwheat, are a preferred choice in the colder and harsher north-eastern regions. Indeed, in 722, soba was planted as an emergency supplementary grain when the rice crop failed – it is a perfect follow-on crop after rice as it takes just 75 days from sowing to harvesting.

Noodles are among the most popular foods in Japan. They are eaten everywhere at any time of the day – as a breakfast substitute at a busy railway station, a quick lunch in Tokyo's business district or a late-night snack after drinking in the Roppongi entertainment area. They are instantly satisfying and easy to digest. Noodles contain carbohydrate, protein, vitamins and minerals. They have very little flavour of their own, so they are an ideal ingredient to cook with others. I hope to demonstrate that Japanese noodles make tasty, easy-to-prepare and above all, comforting and nourishing dishes. All the recipes in this chapter are designed to serve 2.

# How to make noodle dipping sauce

This is a useful and versatile sauce that can be made in advance in a large quantity. The sauce will keep for 2–3 weeks in the fridge in a glass jar. Provided you have used good-quality konbu, shiitake mushrooms and bonito flakes, there is enough flavour left in these ingredients after making the dipping sauce to give taste to another dish: I make a condiment that is delicious and a healthy accompaniment for plain boiled rice. Thinly slice the konbu and shiitake mushrooms and put them in a saucepan with 200ml water, 1 tablespoon soy sauce and ¹/₂ tablespoon mirin. Cook over a gentle heat until nearly all the water has evaporated. Repeat this process three times to intensify the flavour. You should end up with a dark shiny mixture of seaweed and mushrooms. It keeps for up to 1 month in an airtight container in the fridge.

*2 postcard-sized pieces of konbu*
  *(kelp seaweed)*
*4 dried shiitake mushrooms*
*1.2 litres water*
*200ml mirin*
*100ml sake*
*100ml soy sauce*
*1¹/₂ teaspoons sea salt*
*30g bonito flakes*

In a large glass bowl, put the konbu and mushrooms in the measured water and leave to infuse in the fridge overnight.

Put the mirin and sake in a large saucepan and bring to the boil over a high heat. Reduce the heat and cook for 2–3 minutes to burn off the alcohol. Add the soy sauce and return to the boil over a high heat. Add the fish flakes once the liquid reaches the boil, then reduce the heat and continue simmering for 5 minutes.

Let the sauce cool to room temperature before straining it through a sieve lined with kitchen paper. Put the sauce in a sterilised glass jar and store in the fridge.

# Mushroom soba in broth

In cold weather, it is truly comforting to eat a hot bowl of noodles. It is instantly satisfying and warms you up from inside. Japanese mushrooms such as shiitake, shimeji and enoki have become increasingly easy to buy in the West. Mushrooms have many beneficial health properties – they lower blood pressure, reduce cholesterol, are anti-carcinogenic and rich in fibre.

*200g dried soba noodles*
*100ml noodle dipping sauce*
  *(see page 140)*
*750ml water*
*400g assorted mushrooms*
  *of your choice, cleaned and*
  *prepared*
*4 spring onions, finely chopped*
  *diagonally*
*2 tablespoons toasted sesame*
  *seeds, coarsely ground*
*shichimi togarashi (Japanese*
  *seven-spice seasoning)*

**serves 2**

Bring a large saucepan of water to the boil over a high heat. Add the soba noodles and give a quick stir to ensure the noodle strands are separated. Let the water return to the boil and reduce the heat to moderate.

When the water is about to boil over, add a glass of cold water and let it boil again – this is to ensure both the outer and central parts of the noodle strands are cooked at the same speed. When the water returns to the boil for the third time, drain the noodles and rinse them under cold running water. Drain well and set aside.

In a saucepan, heat the noodle dipping sauce and measured water to make a broth. You may vary the amount of water to suit your taste.

When the broth reaches the boil, briefly submerge the noodles to reheat. You may do this with the noodles in a sieve. Divide the warm noodles between two warmed bowls.

Add the mushrooms to the broth and cook for 2–3 minutes. Ladle the broth over the noodles and add the chopped spring onions and sesame seeds. Serve, with the shichimi togarashi offered separately.

# Soba noodle salad with smoked salmon, salmon roe and grated daikon

Refreshing grated daikon (Japanese white radish) works as a bridge between the oily smoked salmon and the soba noodles. I recommend using green tea soba noodles for this recipe – it looks prettier. Dried soba noodles often come in bundles tied together with a thin paper ribbon. Each bundle is one serving, if you are hungry.

*200g dried soba noodles*
  *(preferably green tea variety)*

*400g daikon (Japanese white*
  *radish)*

*4 tablespoons salmon roe*
  *(from a jar)*

*1 tablespoon sake*

*½ white onion, thinly sliced and*
  *soaked in water*

*100ml noodle dipping sauce*
  *(see page 140)*

*100g smoked salmon,*
  *roughly torn*

*4 teaspoons wasabi powder,*
  *mixed with 2 teaspoons water*

*serves 2*

Cook the noodles as described on page 141.

Meanwhile, grate the daikon and reserve both the juice and the grated daikon. Put the salmon roe in a small bowl and pour over the sake – this will take the fishy smell away and separate the roe. Drain the sliced white onion.

Mix the reserved juice of the grated daikon with the dipping sauce – you may vary the amount of the dipping sauce to suit your taste. Divide the noodles between two shallow bowls. Arrange the daikon, smoked salmon pieces, onion slices and salmon roe on top of the noodles. Put a small mound of wasabi paste on top, pour over the dipping sauce mixture and serve.

**Cook's tip**
Try adding some watercress as a garnish – it works wonders.

# Sobagetti with crispy bacon and spinach

A number of my friends have given up eating wheat for various reasons. Soba noodles are made of buckwheat flour, which is gluten-free and provides a healthy and tasty alternative to pasta.

*200g dried soba noodles*

*4 tablespoons olive oil*

*4–6 rashers streaky bacon, chopped*

*1 garlic clove, peeled and crushed*

*100g spinach, roughly chopped*

*4 tablespoons soy sauce*

*salt and black pepper*

serves 2

Cook the soba noodles as described on page 141. Heat a large frying pan and add the olive oil and sauté the bacon bits until they become crispy. Reduce the heat to low and cook the garlic to infuse for 2–3 minutes before adding the spinach. When the spinach becomes wilted, add the soy sauce and adjust the seasoning with salt and pepper. Turn off the heat, add the noodles and toss. Divide the noodle mixture into two pasta dishes and serve.

**Cook's tip**

You can use any green vegetables such as broccoli or rocket leaves. It will give added interest if you can get hold of Japanese greens such as mizuna, mibuna or shungiku, which are increasingly popular.

# Hijiki pasta

Hijiki, like other types of seaweed, is very healthy. It is particularly rich in calcium, magnesium and iron. It is especially popular amongst middle-aged women for its effectiveness against osteoporosis. It is also believed to have a calming effect and promote a good night's sleep. I was never keen on hijiki when I was young but as I get older, I try to emulate how my mother and aunts used to eat.

*50g dried hijiki (seaweed)*

*400g dried udon noodles*

*4 tablespoons olive oil*

*3 garlic cloves, peeled and crushed*

*1 large red chilli, seeded and finely chopped*

*6 anchovy fillets, mashed*

*salt and black pepper*

serves 2

Soak the dried hijiki in plenty of water for 15 minutes and drain well. Bring a large saucepan of water to the boil and add the noodles. When the water returns to the boil and begins to boil over, add a cup of cold water. Let the water return to the boil for the third time and take it off the heat, rinse the noodles under cold running water. Drain well and set aside.

Heat a frying pan over a moderate heat and add the olive oil, then add the garlic and fry until the oil is infused. Add the hijiki, chopped chilli and anchovies. Add the noodles and toss well. Adjust the seasoning with salt and pepper and serve.

# Udon salad with sweet vinegar miso dressing

I often use noodles instead of potatoes for salads, especially in the summer. Although udon noodles are used for this recipe, you may experiment with your favourite noodle.

200g dried udon noodles

2 free-range eggs

200–300g salad leaves of
  your choice

½ cucumber

1 medium carrot

3–4 baby vine tomatoes, halved

**for the salad dressing**

2 tablespoons toasted sesame
  seeds

4 tablespoons sweet vinegar
  miso (see page 169)

1 tablespoon noodle dipping
  sauce (see page 140)

2–3 tablespoons water

**serves 2**

Cook the noodles as described on page 146.

Meanwhile, hard-boil the eggs, shell and slice them.

For the dressing, grind the sesame seeds with a pestle and mortar until they become a coarse paste. Add the rest of the dressing ingredients and mix well.

Tear the salad leaves into manageable-sized pieces. Halve the cucumber and carrot lengthways and slice diagonally.

Place the noodles on a large serving platter and add the salad leaves. Arrange the cucumber, carrot, sliced hard-boiled eggs and tomatoes on top. Drizzle with the salad dressing and serve.

# Beef and leek udon noodle soup

This is a wholesome gutsy noodle soup guaranteed to warm up the body and soul in the cold winter months. Because the authentic recipe calls for a variety of spring onion with a long white stalk, which is available only from Japanese groceries, I have used leeks instead. Spring onions and leeks share similar health properties of warming the body. I often make this dish when I feel that I'm coming down with a cold.

200g dried udon noodles

1 tablespoon vegetable oil

150g silverside or topside of beef, thinly cut

1 medium leek, finely cut diagonally

1 thumb-sized piece of fresh ginger, peeled and cut into matchstick-sized pieces

100ml noodle dipping sauce (see page 140)

600ml water

2 tablespoons medium-coloured miso paste

sansho pepper

serves 2

Cook the noodles in a large saucepan of boiling water for 2–3 minutes. Add a glass of cold water when it is about to boil over. Let the water return to the boil and cook for a further 2–3 minutes. Rinse thoroughly under cold running water and drain well.

Put a saucepan over a moderate heat, add the vegetable oil and sauté the beef and leek. Add the ginger, dipping sauce and water – you may vary the amount of water to suit your taste. Add the miso paste gradually to ensure it dissolves completely. Add the noodles and continue to heat for a further 2–3 minutes, but do not let the liquid boil as this will spoil the miso flavour. Divide the noodle soup between two serving bowls and offer with sansho pepper.

**Cook's tip**

I will let you into a secret about how to stop meat from sticking to the bottom of a pan. Heat the pan and oil in the usual way and then cool the base of the pan by wiping it with a cold damp cloth. But take care not to burn your hand.

# Chilled tomato somen

This recipe was born when we were staying in a farmhouse in Umbria in Italy. The old gardener, with a weather-beaten face like a well-worn brogue shoe, spoke no English and my Italian was equally limited. But he gave me a handful of odd-shaped ripe tomatoes from the garden so I decided to put them together with somen noodles I had brought with us and it was delicious.

500g very ripe vine tomatoes

1 garlic clove (preferably fresh garlic), peeled and grated

1/2 teaspoon salt

1 1/2 tablespoons soy sauce

3–4 tablespoons extra virgin olive oil

200g dried somen noodles

plenty of freshly ground black pepper

fresh basil and flat-leaf parsley, cut into fine strips

serves 2

Blanch the tomatoes in boiling water to skin them. Halve them and discard the seeds. Roughly chop them and mix with the grated garlic, salt, soy sauce and olive oil. Refrigerate the tomato sauce while you cook the somen noodles.

Bring a saucepan of water to the boil and add the noodles. Stir to ensure that the noodles stay separate. Add a glass of cold water when the water is about to boil over. Return to the boil, drain and rinse under cold running water. In a large mixing bowl toss the noodles with the tomato sauce. Divide the noodles between two serving plates and season with pepper. Garnish with the fresh herbs and serve.

# hotpots

**The Japanese** have such a fondness for *Nabe ryori*, the table-top hotpot cooking style for which every region, prefecture and even family has its own favourite recipe. Hotpots are particularly popular during the cold months for birthday celebrations, family gatherings, school reunions and office parties. Like fondues, hotpots are for fun and sociable occasions when everyone joins in and cooking is simple and done at the table. In Japanese there is a term *nabe bugyo*, or 'hotpot sheriff', which describes a person who takes charge of the cooking – it is an affectionate term for husbands and fathers who don't normally enter the kitchen but regard themselves as handy cooks.

It was hard to choose just four recipes for this section since there are literally hundreds but the ones I have selected are all easy to follow and versatile. I recommend that you start with these recipes and, once you feel confident enough, adjust them to suit your own taste and preference. You will need a portable hob and a flameproof pot for these recipes.

**Four basic rules for a 'hotpot sheriff'**

**1** Keep it simple. Decide on a main ingredient, be it vegetables, meat, chicken or seafood. It is tempting to put all your favourites in together, but the tastes of a hotpot easily become blurred and confused.

**2** Do not skimp on preparation. The simplicity of the actual cooking means the preparation of the ingredients will really affect the final result. Not only is the preparation important for taste, but it also makes the dish more appetising to look at and easier to eat.

**3** Waste not, want not. The soup left at the end is full of flavour – do not waste it, but use it to make another course by adding some cooked rice or noodles to round off a sumptuous meal.

**4** Always have larger quantities of the raw ingredients than you think you will need. I am amazed and delighted by the sudden increase in people's appetite when they can participate in cooking for and serving themselves.

# Salmon hotpot

This hotpot originates in the Ishikari region of the northern island of Hokkaido. Hokkaido is a cross between the Scottish Highlands and the Wild West. Its barren rugged landscape resembles some parts of the Scottish Highlands and the Ishikari region is particularly famous for its wild salmon. During the nineteenth century, the government encouraged farmers and miners to move north to open up the frontier and even today the islanders retain an adventurous pioneering spirit and see themselves as separate from the rest of the country. This is a gutsy wholesome hotpot guaranteed to warm up your body and soul.

625g salmon fillet

2 tablespoons sake

200g waxy potatoes, cleaned

2 medium carrots, peeled

1 sweetcorn cob

500g Chinese cabbage

2 medium leeks, trimmed

4 shiitake mushrooms, stalks
   removed

2 tablespoons butter

for the seasoning sauce

1 litre dashi stock
   (see pages 16–17)

80g medium-coloured miso paste

2 tablespoons soy sauce

2 tablespoons sake

2 tablespoons mirin

**Preparation**  Cut the salmon fillet into bite-sized pieces, pour over the sake and set aside.

Steam or boil the potatoes in their skins and cut them into bite-sized pieces. Cut the carrots into big chunks. Quarter the corn cob. Cut the cabbage into bite-sized pieces. Cut the leeks diagonally into chunky pieces. Arrange all the vegetables on a large platter.

In a large jar, mix all the ingredients for the seasoning sauce and stir well to ensure the miso paste is dissolved.

**At the table**  Put a cooking pot on a portable hob at the centre of the table. Put all the seasoning sauce in the pot and bring to the boil over a high heat. Add all the other ingredients to the pot when the sauce begins to boil, reduce the heat and let it simmer for 10–15 minutes or until the potatoes are soft. Add the butter and invite the guests to help themselves.

# Zen tofu hotpot

I first had this dish at a Zen temple in Kyoto on a chilly autumn day. Although I was only ten years old, the purity and warm sensation of the tofu has remained with me ever since. The authentic recipe calls for the highest-quality tofu that is, sadly, not available outside Japan – so I have added shimeji mushrooms for a bit of extra taste.

**for the konbu stock**

1 approximately A4-sized piece
   of konbu (dried kelp seaweed)
500g firm cotten tofu
100g shimeji mushrooms

**for the dipping sauce**

100ml soy sauce
25ml mirin
100ml water
25g bonito flakes
2 spring onions, finely chopped
zest of ½ lemon
2 teaspoons red chilli flakes
   (optional)

**Preparation**  For the konbu stock, soak the konbu in 1.5 litres water overnight to infuse the konbu's umami (the fifth primary taste).

With a pair of chopsticks, cut the tofu into bite-sized cubes – the reason for using the chopsticks instead of a knife is to leave rough edges so that the sauce has more tofu surface to cling to. Separate the shimeji mushrooms. Arrange the tofu and mushrooms on a large platter.

Put all the ingredients for the dipping sauce in a saucepan, bring to the boil over a moderate heat and strain.

**At the table**  Place a portable hob at the centre of the table and put a cooking pot on top. Each guest should have a bowl of dipping sauce. Fill the cooking pot halfway up with the prepared konbu stock and turn on the heat. When the stock begins to boil, add the remaining tofu and mushrooms. Reduce the heat to low to simmer for 5 minutes or so, then invite the guests to help themselves. Replenish the pot with tofu and mushrooms as they are eaten.

**Hotpot sheriff's tip**

If you have a small heat-resistant jug, fill it with the dipping sauce and place it in the centre of the cooking pot. This will keep the dipping sauce warm.

# Vegetarian hotpot

This is a simple yet tasty vegetarian dish. There are no strict rules as to what you can put in – but try to balance the tastes, textures and colours. Think of this as a warm vegetable salad. I am also suggesting three varieties of dipping sauce to enjoy.

4 deep-fried tofu blocks

konbu stock (see page 152)

400g daikon (Japanese white
   radish), peeled

1 carrot, peeled

2 medium turnips, peeled

**for the hot chilli soy
dipping sauce**

100ml sake

200ml soy sauce

3 large red chillies

3 large green chillies

½ lemon

**sesame and sweet miso
dipping  sauce**

4 tablespoons toasted sesame
   seeds

4 tablespoons sweet vinegar
   miso dressing (see page 169)

4 tablespoons noodle dipping
   sauce (see page 140)

100ml water

citrus soy dipping sauce
   (see page 154)

**Preparation** Blanch the deep-fried tofu in a saucepan of boiling water for 1 minute to rid it of any excess oil. Cut the leek diagonally. Arrange all the vegetables with the tofu on a large platter.

For the hot chilli soy dipping sauce, boil the sake in a saucepan to burn off the alcohol and add the soy sauce. Allow it to return to the boil, then let it cool to room temperature. Meanwhile, make incisions lengthways in the chillies and slice the lemon. Put them in a sterilised jar and pour over the soy mixture when it has cooled down. Refrigerate and use within 4 weeks.

For the sesame and sweet miso dipping sauce, grind the sesame seeds with a pestle and mortar until smooth. Add the rest of the ingredients and grind to incorporate.

**At the table**  Place a cooking pot on a portable hob at the centre of the table. Fill the pot with the konbu stock and add about half of the ingredients and bring to the boil over a high heat. Reduce the heat to low and offer the hotpot with the three varieties of dipping sauce. Replenish the vegetables as required.

# Chicken hotpot

Slow simmering brings out all the goodness and flavour of chicken – make sure you use the best-quality organic birds for this dish. I recommend citrus-flavoured soy sauce for dipping – and why not add some cooked rice and beaten eggs to the wonderful cooking juices left at the end to make a comforting rice porridge?

625g chicken thighs with bones

500g Chinese cabbage

1–2 medium leeks

1–2 medium carrots, peeled

100g shimeji or oyster
    mushrooms

**for the chicken stock**

1 chicken carcass, washed

2 litres dashi stock
    (see pages 16–17)

100ml sake

**for the citrus soy
dipping sauce**

100ml grapefruit juice

100ml yuzu juice (available in
    bottles from Japanese stores)
    or lime juice

100ml soy sauce

**Preparation**  For the chicken stock, put the washed chicken carcass in a large saucepan with the dashi stock and sake and bring to the boil over a high heat. Reduce the heat and continue to simmer for a further 30 minutes, skimming off any scum that floats to the surface. Take out the chicken and strain the stock; set the stock aside until cooking starts.

Blanch the chicken thighs in a saucepan of boiling water for 5 minutes, drain and rinse in cold water. Chop the Chinese cabbage into bite-sized pieces. Chop the leeks and carrots diagonally. Separate the shimeji mushrooms. Arrange the vegetables on a large platter.

For the citrus soy dipping sauce, mix all the ingredients together and then divide into dipping bowls.

**At the table**  Place a portable hob at the centre of the table with a cooking pot on top. Each guest should have a bowl of dipping sauce. Fill the cooking pot halfway with the prepared stock and bring it to the boil over a high heat. Put in about a third of the prepared chicken thighs and allow the stock to return to the boil before adding a third of the vegetables. Reduce the heat to low and simmer for about 10–15 minutes until the vegetables are soft, then invite the guests to help themselves. Replenish the stock, chicken and vegetables as needed.

# sweet

**When I first** came to England it took me a while to appreciate the significance of dessert or pudding, which is nearly always sweet or chocolate-flavoured and served at the end of a meal. In the context of a Western-style meal, dessert occupies as important a position as a starter or main course. In contrast, a traditional Japanese meal ends with a bowl of rice, miso soup and pickles. A few slices of seasonal fruits described as *mizu gashi* (literally, water sweets) are often served after the rice and soup, but this is not considered as a part of the meal.

Yet the Japanese are fond of confectionary of all kinds. They distinguish between *yogashi* (Western-style confectionary) and *wagashi* (Japanese-style). A typical indigenous confection is made from fruits, root vegetables, beans, nuts, seeds, seaweeds and rice products and never uses any dairy products. These traditional confections are consumed either at tea ceremonies or as *oyatsu* – meaning honourable eight,

they are eaten as a mid-afternoon snack at the eighth hour on the traditional Japanese clock system – the equivalent of two o'clock in the afternoon. The relatively recent origin of *oyatsu* dates back only to the seventeenth century. Today, as cross-cultural influences become ever more prominent, serving dessert to round off a meal, Japanese or non-Japanese, has become an established custom. However, the practice of taking a mid-afternoon snack with tea lives on in Japan in harmony with the adopted Western tradition of serving dessert at the end of the meal.

Choosing dessert recipes for this book proved more challenging than any other chapter because the notion of dessert and the role played by sweets is so different in our two cultures. I have tried and, I hope, succeeded in accommodating the expectations of Western diners by selecting recipes that will provide the sense of a treat to round off a meal while preserving the integrity of the traditional Japanese confection.

# Dorayaki – pancake with sweet adzuki bean paste

This is so named because in appearance it resembles a *dorayaki*, or copper gong used in Buddhist ceremonies and court music. Provided you have a good supply of home-made sweet adzuki bean paste, it is very easy and quick to make.

1 medium free-range egg
  and 1 egg yolk
75g caster sugar
1 teaspoon runny honey
1/2 teaspoon bicarbonate of soda
40ml water
100g plain flour
1 tablespoon vegetable oil
175g sweet adzuki bean paste
  (see page 158)

**makes approximately
12 pancakes**

In a bowl, beat the egg and egg yolk lightly and sift in the caster sugar. Continue to beat the egg mixture until it turns pale yellow. Add the honey and mix well.

In a separate bowl, dissolve the bicarbonate of soda with half of the water and add to the egg mixture. Hold the sieve above the egg mixture, sift in the flour and, with a cut-and-turn motion, fold the flour into the egg mixture. Do not overstir the mixture. Cover the bowl with clingfilm and refrigerate for 20–30 minutes.

Heat a non-stick frying pan over a moderate heat and add the oil. With a tablespoon, pour the mixture to make an 8cm-wide pancake. When small air bubbles begin to appear, flip it over to cook the other side. Repeat the process to make eleven more pancakes of a similar size. Transfer them on to a rack to cool.

Divide the adzuki paste into six equal portions. Spread the paste on half of the pancakes and top each with a second pancake to sandwich the paste. Eat within 3 days of making.

# Adzuki bean paste

Adzuki bean paste is the most important ingredient used in making *wagashi* – traditional Japanese confections. It is comfortingly sweet but has all the nutritious goodness of adzuki beans including iron, kalium and edible fibre. These beans are most valuable nutritionally for anti-oxidation property that prevents high blood pressure and other lifestyle-related conditions as well as cancer. Although ready-made varieties are available in tins, home-made adzuki bean paste is always better and it is not difficult to prepare, just time-consuming. So I suggest you cook a large amount when you have some spare time and keep it refrigerated.

There are two types of paste, grainy and smooth. The recipe is mostly the same until the beans are blended in a food processor. Smooth adzuki bean paste is like a soft silken tofu in contrast to the more robust firm cotton tofu. It is delectably silky, delicate and subtly sweet. Refrigerate both pastes in an airtight container and use within three weeks or, alternatively, freeze in small batches.

## For the grainy variety

*300g dried adzuki beans*
*200g granulated sugar*
*pinch of salt*

**makes approximately 750g**

Put the beans in a sieve, discard any imperfect ones and rinse under cold running water – handle them gently. Place the beans in a heavy-based saucepan, add 600ml water and bring to the boil over a moderate heat. Add another 200ml water to reduce the temperature to soften the beans. Let it return to the boil and simmer for 2 minutes before turning off the heat. Drain and rinse under cold running water. Clean the saucepan and return the beans with 800ml water; bring to the boil again over a moderate heat. Keep adding more water to maintain the water temperature just below boiling point and continue to simmer for 10 minutes or until the wrinkles on the beans disappear. Drain the beans in a sieve and rinse under cold running water.

Clean the saucepan again and return the beans with 850ml water. Put the saucepan over a moderate/high heat to bring to the boil and lower the heat to simmer for 45–60 minutes. Try to maintain the simmering temperature by adding water from time to time – do not stir at all as it will make the beans go hard. Take a spoonful of beans to test their softness and if you can squash them between your fingers without too much effort they are done. Transfer the beans into a sieve and put them in a bowl with some of the cooking liquid. Blend the mixture in a food processor, in 2–3 batches, and give each batch 10–20 seconds of whizzing. The paste should have a grainy texture with many of the beans still recognisable.

Put half of the bean paste in a large saucepan with the sugar and heat rapidly over a high heat, stirring with a wooden spoon until the liquid starts to boil. Reduce the heat to moderate/low, add the rest of the bean paste and continue to stir, taking care not to let it burn at the bottom, until most of the liquid has evaporated. Add the salt and stir well. Turn off the heat and spread the paste on a large plate to cool. Refrigerate once it has reached room temperature.

## For the smooth variety

Process the beans until you have a smooth paste. Place a fine sieve over a large bowl and, with plenty of water, wash off the skins of the beans in small batches. Discard the skins, add more water to fill the bowl and stir gently. Leave to stand for a few minutes to let the mixture settle. By gently tilting the bowl, drain off the top cloudy layer. Repeat this blanching until the water becomes clear. This blanching process is important as it determines the taste of the final bean paste.

Place a clean piece of muslin or tea towel over a bowl and gently pour over the bean mixture to drain the water. You should be left with a dry, smooth bean mash. Put 70ml water and the sugar in a saucepan and heat until all the sugar has dissolved. Add half of the bean mash and bring it to the boil over a rapid heat, stirring all the time to avoid burning – add more water if it is too dry. The consistency you are trying to achieve is not dissimilar to that of cream cheese. The continuous stirring is important as it makes the paste creamier and elastic. When the paste has achieved the desired consistency, spread it on a tray and leave to cool.

# Green tea ice cream and adzuki paste

This is one of my darkest secret cheat recipes. As there is no tradition of desserts to round off a meal in Japan, I used to, and still do to some extent, find it difficult and often run out of time to prepare a good dessert when I am giving a dinner party. This is my trump card – it is the easiest recipe in this entire book and is a downright cheat with a satisfyingly good result. You need a high-quality vanilla ice cream.

325g very good-quality vanilla
    ice cream of your choice
2 teaspoons matcha (green
    tea) powder
1 teaspoon tepid water
4 tablespoons home-made sweet
    adzuki bean paste
    (see pages 158–159)

Start with softening the ice cream by taking it out of the freezer and transferring it to the fridge for 15–20 minutes – but do not let it melt.

Put the matcha powder in a small, fine-meshed sieve or a tea strainer held over a mixing bowl and push it through. Use the back of a teaspoon to ensure all the tea powder is used. Gently add the tepid water and mix well.

Add half of the ice cream and mix thoroughly with a rubber spatula. Then add the rest of the ice cream. You can stop mixing when the ice cream looks marbled or you may continue mixing to achieve a uniform pale-green-coloured ice cream. Place the bowl in the freezer for 45–60 minutes to harden the ice cream.

This amount makes eight scoops. Serve each with 1/2 tablespoon of the adzuki bean paste.

**Cook's tip**
You can make another Japanese-inspired ice cream by using the sweet adzuki bean paste (see pages 158–159) to mix in with the vanilla ice cream.

# Seasonal fruit jewellery box

You may vary the choice of fruits in this recipe to suit your taste and what is seasonally available, but try to use a variety of appealing colours so that the fruits captured in the jelly resemble shimmering jewels.

1/2 honeydew melon, peeled and
  cut into small cubes
200g watermelon, deseeded
  and cut into small cubes
2 Japanese medlars, peeled,
  stoned and cut into small
  cubes (or substitute with an
  orange-coloured fruit such
  as papaya)
1 peach or nectarine, peeled,
  stoned and cubed
8 seedless white grapes
8 seedless dark grapes
12 blueberries
4 tablespoons mirin
2 tablespoons yuzu juice or
  lime juice
600ml water
4 tablespoons sugar
2 teaspoons gelatine, soaked in
  cold water

Put all the fruits in a mixing bowl, pour over the mirin and yuzu or lime juice and mix well to coat the fruits with the liquid.

Select four small bowls or coffee cups. Cut four small squares of clingfilm and use to line the small bowls or cups to create moulds. Divide the fruit evenly between them.

Heat the measured water, the sugar and gelatine in a saucepan over a moderate heat to just below boiling point. Stir continuously with a wooden spoon, scraping the bottom of the saucepan to prevent the mixture from scorching. Take it off the heat and cool by placing the saucepan in a bowl of ice-cold water.

When the gelatine mixture begins to thicken, pour it on top of the diced fruit in the moulds, gather the clingfilm to create small bundles and refrigerate until the gelatine sets.

Turn out the fruit jellies, gently remove the clingfilm and serve, either wrapped in bamboo-leaf cups or placed directly in attractive glass dishes.

# How to make a perfect cup of green tea

In Japan, tea is drunk all day from breakfast time to dinner in the evening. If you go to any business meeting, you will be automatically presented with a cup of tea. All hotel rooms in Japan are equipped with tea-making equipment. In a restaurant, your tea cup will be constantly topped up. It is inconceivable to have a meal without tea. In other words, tea is drunk all the time, everywhere.

Freshly picked tea leaves are immediately steamed to prevent discolouring and fermentation, then dried by rolling and crumbling and finally by hot air. The colour, aroma and shape of the leaves define the quality of the tea. Japanese green tea should not be brewed with boiling-hot water, and the better the quality of tea, the lower the temperature of the water used. Here I have listed five varieties of tea drunk with or without a meal.

### Gyokuro

Its name meaning 'jewel dew', this is the highest-quality tea made from young tender leaves picked in early spring. The tea leaves are highly fragrant and a deep shiny green. The tea should be brewed in warm water of about 50°C in small amounts. It is drunk on its own or accompanied with *wagashi* (Japanese sweets), but not with a meal. Brew it for no more than 2–3 minutes.

### Sencha

This literally means 'infused tea'. It is a middle-ranking, good everyday tea drunk at home. The tea should be brewed in water of about 60°C. Used tea leaves can be reused for a second time, but use slightly hotter water.

### Bancha

This is an everyday, ordinary drinking tea served freely in restaurants and offices. It is made of larger leaves and stems and makes a yellowish green tea. There are varying qualities of bancha and, the lower the grade, the more stems and even twigs are included.

### Hojicha

This is a roasted bancha with a nutty, woody flavour. It is the tea most often drunk with a meal, especially breakfast. Although you can buy this from Japanese grocery stores, you can make it at home by dry-toasting bancha.

### Genmaicha

This is a mixture of bancha and toasted rice grains which has a nutty aroma and mild flavour.

# sauces and dressings

**A good friend** of mine who was then a head chef of a famous Japanese restaurant in London winked and told me once that 'it is all in the sauce', as he applied professional finishing touches to my dish. Indeed there were more than two dozen sauces and dressings all ready to be used in squeezy plastic bottles on a large tray. I watched him selecting one as if he were an artist carefully choosing his paints.

Sauces and dressings are essentially a way of adding more flavour and sometimes an additional texture. They provide another layer, giving a dish extra depth and character. I have always regarded sauces, marinades and dressings rather like accessories, making sometimes dramatic and at other times subtle changes to a simple black dress. Of course, a home cook is not expected to compete with professionals, but a few carefully selected home-made sauces and dressings will expand your cooking repertoire enormously and help to cut down on time spent cooking, so that you can enjoy the delicious results with your family and friends. This chapter should be used in tandem with the earlier section on soy sauce, vinegar, miso, sake and mirin (pages 12–13). In Japanese cooking, those five ingredients provide the platform of basic taste and flavour. Making a sauce is a matter of combining those seasoning ingredients. It is tempting to use everything you like, from soy sauce to sweet mirin or spicy chilli, but my advice is to keep it simple – decide which of the basic flavours you wish to build on and do not confuse it by adding too many conflicting seasoning ingredients. As your confidence increases, I am sure that you will be soon developing your own sauces and dressings, but here are some recipes to start with.

## Teriyaki sauce

After soy sauce, teriyaki sauce must be the most popular and widely used sauce in Japanese cooking. Although it is possible to buy ready-made versions, home-made teriyaki is always better, more economical and healthier because you know what went into it. I always make a large quantity and divide it into four, keeping one plain and infusing the others with garlic, chilli and ginger.

75ml soy sauce
75ml sake
75ml mirin
25g sugar (you may vary the amount to suit your taste)

Put all the ingredients in a wide shallow saucepan over a moderate heat and stir to ensure that the sugar dissolves. Bring to the boil, then lower the heat to simmer until the sauce has reduced by a quarter. Let it cool down completely before storing in a glass jar with a lid.

To make the garlic-infused sauce, peel a whole clove, bruise it slightly with the blade of your kitchen knife and place it in the teriyaki sauce while it is still warm. For the chilli-infused sauce, make an incision lengthways in a large red chilli and then place it in the still-warm sauce. For the ginger-infused sauce, peel a thumb-sized piece of fresh ginger, bruise it slightly and put it in the still-warm sauce.

**Cook's tip**
Teriyaki sauce will keep, if refrigerated, for up to 3 weeks, but the initial nutty aroma will deteriorate after a while.

## Dashi joyu

This is my most useful sauce of all time – there is always a jar in my fridge. I use it as a noodle dipping sauce, marinade, or cooking liquid for rice, or simply pour it over a chilled block of tofu. It is highly versatile. It is not as strongly flavoured as pure soy sauce but more subtle and more flavoursome than ordinary dashi stock.

5cm x 5cm piece of konbu (kelp seaweed)
120ml mirin
50ml sake
100ml soy sauce
5g dried bonito flakes

Put a non-stick frying pan over a low heat and dry-toast the konbu piece to enhance its flavour. Put the mirin and sake in a saucepan over a moderate heat and bring to the boil to burn off the alcohol. Add the soy sauce and return to the boil before turning off the heat. Add the dried bonito flakes and set aside to cool.

Line a sieve with a piece of kitchen paper and strain the liquid. Transfer into a storage jar and add the konbu. Do not refrigerate, but let the konbu infuse for 2–3 days before use.

**Cook's tip**
You can turn this into a refreshing salad dressing by adding grated daikon (Japanese white radish). Or you can make a Japanese barbecue sauce by adding tomato ketchup and grated garlic.

## Yunan miso – citrus miso

It is hard to choose one miso-based sauce from endless variations, but I think this recipe is one of the most versatile and has an excellent rich citrus flavour. You can use this recipe as a salad dressing, marinade, coating sauce for steamed vegetables, barbecue sauce or even as a dip with a difference.

*100ml sake*
*100ml mirin*
*300g white or light-coloured miso paste*
*4 tablespoons light soy sauce*
*50ml yuzu juice or lime juice*

Put the sake and mirin in a saucepan over a high heat, bring to the boil and cook for 2 minutes to burn off the alcohol. Turn off the heat and add the miso paste, little by little, stirring well with an egg whisk to ensure all the miso is dissolved. Add the soy sauce and yuzu or lime juice and allow to cool completely before storing in a glass jar.

**Cook's tip**

This miso mixture works wonderfully as a marinade – try marinating salmon fillets or mackerel overnight with it. Wipe off the miso well before grilling the fish. It also makes an excellent salad dressing: dilute it with, preferably, dashi stock, or just water to preferred consistency.

## Sanbaizu – savoury sweet vinegar

In Japanese cooking, vinegar plays many important but often hidden roles – it is used to draw out excess moisture and odour, it highlights umami and subtly seasons fish or vegetables. For vegetables, vinegar is used to freshen both the texture and colour. *Sanbaizu* is one of the three classic vinegar blends, which is flavoured with soy sauce and bonito flakes and is mildly sweetened with sugar. It can be used on its own like a salad dressing, as a seasoning for steamed vegetables or served with deep- or shallow-fried food.

*225ml rice vinegar*
*75g sugar*
*75ml soy sauce*
*5g dried bonito flakes*

Put all the ingredients, except the fish flakes, in a saucepan and bring to the boil over a moderate heat. Stir to ensure that all the sugar is dissolved. Turn off the heat, add the bonito fish flakes and allow to infuse while cooling. Line a fine sieve with a piece of kitchen paper to strain the vinegar mixture. Refrigerate and use within 2 weeks.

**Cook's tip**

I put a few strips of konbu (dried kelp seaweed) in the bottle of rice vinegar so that the vinegar is naturally infused with the konbu's umami. As in the case of teriyaki sauce, try chilli or garlic to add extra flavour to the sanbaizu.

# sweet vinegar miso dressing

75ml sake
200g white or light-coloured
   miso paste
75g sugar
100ml rice vinegar

Put the sake in a saucepan, bring to the boil over a high heat and cook for 2 minutes to burn off the alcohol. Reduce the heat to moderate/low and add the rest of the ingredients. Cook for 5–7 minutes, stirring constantly with a wooden spoon. Turn off the heat when all the ingredients are fully combined and the consistency resembles that of thick yogurt. Allow them to cool, store in a glass jar and refrigerate. The dressing keeps for 4–5 weeks.

# Japanese salad dressing

Salads are not in the traditional Japanese repertoire, but to a nation of vegetable lovers salad has become a familiar dish on Japanese tables. The popularity of salads is not hard to understand considering that there are many salad equivalents, such as *sunomono*, vinegar-flavoured dishes, and *aemono*, coated vegetables or fish with various sauces such as tofu or miso paste. These small dishes are treated as side dishes either to whet the appetite or cleanse the palate between courses for which many varieties of vinegar-based sauces are used. This recipe is more of a Western salad dressing, but with a Japanese twist.

2 shallots, peeled and grated
1/2–1 garlic clove, peeled and
   finely grated
50ml rice vinegar
25ml soy sauce
1/2 teaspoon sugar
1 teaspoon grainy mustard
pinch each of salt and pepper
25ml sunflower oil
1 teaspoon sesame oil

Just put all the ingredients in a lidded glass jar and shake it vigorously to mix. Keep refrigerated and use within 2 days.

**Cook's tip**
Try making this with grated daikon (Japanese white radish) instead of shallots, with a few drops of lemon juice for variation.

# The art of serving and presentation

Eating a Japanese meal engages all five senses, not just taste and smell, but first of all the sight of the food, which captures and excites your desire and makes you want to eat. The presentation of food is an integral part of Japanese cuisine. I have already stressed the importance of the four seasons in Japanese cuisine, but the Japanese sensitivity and appreciation of nature's cycle does not end in choosing seasonal ingredients and cooking them in seasonally appropriate methods; it extends to serving and presentation. We aim to bring the seasons directly to the table.

At the beginning of each season, I used to help my mother change not only the tableware but also our clothes, the paintings and the scrolls hung on the walls and ornaments in the house. I remember it always being a happy and exciting occasion that made me aware of and appreciate the cycle of the seasons and the rhythms of nature. In Japan, restaurants and traditional inns have at least four sets of tableware and often many more for different seasonal festive occasions. Even private homes have a wide range of tableware in different materials, shapes, colours and sizes. I am not suggesting that you go out and buy a whole range of

Japanese tableware, but you might perhaps acquire one or two Japanese-inspired platters or bowls and mix them with your existing crockery.

At a Japanese home table, there is no requirement for uniformity of tableware; rather the cook is encouraged to mix and match containers fashioned from a variety of materials – pottery, porcelain, glass, lacquer, wood or bamboo. I also borrow bits of nature – flowers and leaves from the garden, driftwood, pebbles and shells from the beach, red berries and acorns; all these bring a seasonal touch to the table. But remember that the Japanese way is: 'less is more'.

## Serving suggestions

A home cook has to work within the limits of his or her existing tableware, but keeping within these confines often makes you more innovative – it is perfectly possible to create different effects with a single round dinner plate. For example, do not fill the whole plate with food but leave a large area of it uncovered. The art of serving Japanese food

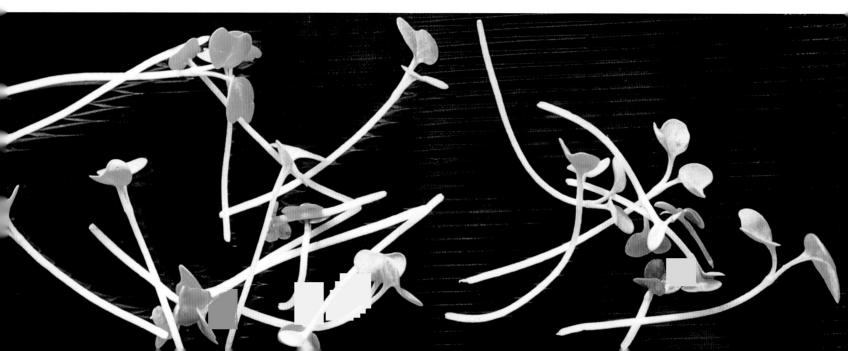

lies in the ability to reflect nature on the plate. You paint a culinary landscape – there is a mountain, a small mound of food and at the foot there is the sea, the cooking liquid or a sauce, and then the sky depicted by the uncovered parts of the plate. The same principle of creating a landscape applies to serving soups. As the photograph of the front cover of this book shows, you can create an island in the centre of a bowl.

You can achieve a harmonious balance on the plate by using food of contrasting colours and shapes. Use the principle of five colours (see page 8) that not only results in a nutritiously balanced dish but also provides contrasting colours on the plate. Do not put the same-coloured vegetables next to each other. The principle also applies to shapes of food – generally, round-shaped food such as rolled sushi or rolled meat looks more interesting if served on square or rectangular plates. If you do not possess different-shaped plates, it is possible to create the shape on a round plate by using a sheet of nori, or a banana leaf, or by drawing a square line with the sauce.

Another serving principle is number – the Japanese prefer odd numbers like three and five, because it is easier to create contrasts with odd numbers than even numbers. We particularly shy away from four, as the sound of the number, *shi*, is the same as the word for death and we consider it a bad omen. Do not serve four pieces or slices of Japanese food. But you don't always have to serve individually – presenting food on a big platter is a practical but dramatic way of serving that never fails to impress your guests. It also allows people to decide how much or how little they wish to take.

The garnish is important; there is a saying in Japan that just as a person can't go out naked, neither can food. Carefully placed shiso leaves or a small sprig of shiso flowers or wasabi paste moulded in a leaf are integral to the art of presentation. In Japan, there is a wide variety of edible garnishes on sale, from leaves to flowers and berries. In the West, we have to be imaginative and use substitutes – sprigs of herbs, cress or halved cherry tomatoes are a good start. I use dandelion flowers in the spring, strawberry flowers in the summer and red maple leaves in the autumn.

The art of presentation and serving is to bring the best out of food you cooked so that it gives the maximum enjoyment to your family and friends.

# Etiquette

**In the relaxed atmosphere** of the home, either at a family meal or even at a dinner party with friends, there is no need to observe strict etiquette or formal table manners other than the most obvious show of appreciation for the food. However, knowing a few basic dos and don'ts of Japanese dining etiquette helps you to relax and ultimately will increase pleasures of eating. So here I have listed some of the essentials, mainly regarding chopsticks.

At the start of a Japanese meal we have the Japanese equivalent of grace – we put our hands together in front of our faces looking at the table and say, 'Itadakimasu', I receive with gratitude. This one word says it all. You don't have to be fluent in Japanese but take a brief moment, with your hands together or not, first look at the food placed before you and engage your visual sense. Next, breathe in the aromas and contemplate the pleasures you are about to experience. It doesn't have to be long, just a minute or two or even a few seconds, but taking a moment before you begin eating prepares you to engage all your senses and truly appreciate the food you are about to receive; it is a gift of nourishment and good health.

If you are given a pair of disposable wooden chopsticks in a paper sleeve, take them out of the sleeve, carefully break them apart and, if there is one, place them on the small chopstick rest in front of you. The same pair is used throughout the meal. Do not wave them around, point at things or chew on the end. If there is no chopstick rest, when you are not using them you should lay them parallel to the edge of the table in front of you. Keeping a pair of chopsticks neatly closed together is rather like sitting properly with your legs together. It certainly makes me feel uncomfortable to see a pair of chopsticks strewn carelessly on the table. If there is no chopstick rest you can have fun in making an origami version with the paper sleeve.

Never stick chopsticks upright into a bowl of rice – it reminds superstitious Japanese of the stands of incense at traditional Japanese funerals. You should also never pass a piece of food to another with your chopsticks because not only is it unhygienic but again it's reminiscent of the Japanese funeral ceremony. If rice is served in a bowl, pick the bowl up with your left hand and hold it closer to eat but don't put your lips to it. And by the way, never, ever pour soy sauce on your rice – keep it clean and unadulterated.

If you are helping yourself from a large communal plate or serving someone else, it is hygienic and polite to turn your chopsticks around and use the top ends.

At the end of a meal, place the pair of chopsticks you have been using neatly in front of you – this symbolises that you are satisfied and nourished by the meal you have just had.

The Japanese equivalent of grace at the end of a meal is 'Gochisosama', I have received with gratitude. Again we say this one word with our hands held together in front of our faces with our heads slightly bowed.

If all this chopstick etiquette sound too much for you, here is one easy rule to remember – hold your cup or glass when someone pours you a drink and return the courtesy by pouring a drink in turn.

Finally, it is alright to slurp when you are eating a bowl of noodles in broth – it is considered showing appreciation. But don't do it when eating soups.

# Composing a Japanese menu

**Principles and examples.** When devising a menu, I try to chart the basic guidelines, which can be followed by drawing on good old common sense. Dishes served side by side should not compete with, but complement each other and work harmoniously to provide a balanced meal. The same principle applies to texture – no one is likely to enjoy a sequence of courses that are equally runny, or dense, or starchy. So always try to provide a harmonious balance in tastes and texture. My advice is to start with cooking one course or a single dish from this book and incorporate it in your existing repertoire rather than embarking on an ambitious Japanese three-course menu. As you gain more confidence in cooking these dishes, gradually expand. It is better to serve one well-cooked and beautifully presented dish than three or more dishes of mediocrity.

## Spring lunch party
Japanese omelette with tomato and chives (page 94)
Smoked salmon, salmon roe and daikon noodle salad (page 143)
Broccoli and scrambled egg sushi (page 134)

## Summer barbecue
Asian gazpacho with coriander pesto (page 31)
Japanese-style chicken hamburgers (page 87) /
Chicken teriyaki (page 91)
Spicy edamame (page 48)/grilled sweetcorn with teriyaki (page 46)
Green salad with Japanese salad dressing (page 169)

## Autumn rustic family supper
Roast pumpkin soup with lime and coriander pesto (page 32)
Simmered sardines in ginger vinegar (page 66)/
Slow-cooked belly of pork (page 105)
Shimeji mushroom and chicken rice (page 130)

## Winter warming dinner
Shredded chicken in dashi broth (page 19)
Pan-sautéd marlin with citrus miso teriyaki sauce (page 73) /

Pot-roasted rack of lamb with rice vinegar (page 108)/
Sake-steamed chicken parcels with pak choi (page 90)
Warm bean sprouts salad with crispy garlic (page 57)

## Fish feast
New sashimi of sea bream with hot oil (page 76)
Oyster congee (page 80)
Wakame and yam salad (page 84)
Green tea ice cream with adzuki bean paste (page 160)

## Vegetarian lunch
Japanese spring cabbage coleslaw (page 37)
Japanese new potato salad with tofu mayo (page 44)
Warm tofu and steamed vegetable salad (page 121)
Hijiki pasta (page 144)

## Vegetarian dinner
Spring vegetable minestrone soup with white miso (page 26)
Zen tofu hotpot (page 152)
Purple-sprouting broccoli with mustard soy (page 36)
Dorayaki (page 157)

## Elegant ladies' lunch
Sea bream in clear dashi broth (page 22)
Cucumber and steamed chicken salad (page 41)
Chilled tomato somen (page 148)

## Celebration dinner
Smoked salmon, salmon roe and capers sushi (page 136)
Chicken hotpot (page 154)
Daikon salad with watercress and walnuts (page 51)

## Romantic supper for two
Vine-ripened tomato soup in red miso (page 24)
Japanese-style beef steak (page 97)
Asparagus and broad bean domburi (page 125)

# Index

## Acknowledgements

My big thank you goes to the team that created this book. The very first thank you is to Kyle Cathie for commissioning, supporting and advising me to make this possible – I thank you for giving me so much room and trust, you are my guiding inspiration. My editor, Sophie Allen for her calm and tireless work in project managing and editing – you made everything seem so easy. To Vanessa Courtier for her long hours behind the scenes designing. Linda Tubby for interpreting my recipes and preparing flawless food. Louise Mackaness for preparing and styling the food for the front cover. Wei Tang for her fine choices in styling and props. Jan Baldwin for taking such beautiful and inviting photos – you are such a sympathetic photographer and made me feel at ease in front of the camera instead of wanting to run away from it.

A huge gratitude goes to my family, my husband Stephen, our three boys, Maxi, Frederick, and Dominic, for their patience, understanding and support while I worked many weekends and their willingness to test many new recipes.

*Arigato* to Mrs. Junko Ohotaki for her enthusiastic support, to her young doctor son, Yuhei for his fine calligraphy and most of all, their warmest friendship. Another big *arigato* goes to Mrs Rie Tada and her late husband.

A big thank you to Rosie and Eric Treuile at London's Mecca for foodies, Books for Cooks, for giving me the initial opportunity for starting my food career and your continued support.

First published in Great Britain in 2006 by
Kyle Cathie Limited, 122 Arlington Road, London NW1 7HP
general.enquiries@kyle-cathie.com   www.kylecathie.com

ISBN 1 85626 665 6    ISBN (13-digit) 978 1 85626 665 9

Text © 2006 by Kimiko Barber
Design © 2006 by Kyle Cathie Limited
Photography © 2006 Jan Baldwin

Edited by Sophie Allen
Art direction and design by Vanessa Courtier
Photography by Jan Baldwin
Home economy by Linda Tubby and Louise Mackaness (front cover, pp 21, 27, 127, 135, 142)
Styling by Wei Tang
Proofreading by Ruth Baldwin
Production by Sha Huxtable and Alice Holloway

Kimiko Barber is hereby identified as the author of this work in accordance with Section 77 of the Copyright, Designs and Patents Act 1988.

A Cataloguing in Publication record for this title is available from the British Library.

Colour reproduction by Colourscan Pty Ltd
Printed in China by C&C Offset Printing Co., Ltd.

**All recipes serve 4, unless otherwise stated.**

**The Japanese characters throughout the book have been chosen to complement the chapters. Here is a translation of what they mean.**

Front cover, page 1 – **well-being**    Cooking in Japan (pages 9, 17) – **beginning**    Soups (pages 18, 25) – **nourishing**
Vegetables (pages 33, 41, 46, 51, 58) – **four seasons**    Fresh from the sea (pages 62, 73, 76, 81, 84) – **sea**
Poultry and eggs (pages 86, 91) – **egg**    Meat (pages 96, 101, 104) – **power**    Tofu and beans (pages 110, 113, 116, 119 ) – **zen**
Rice and Sushi (pages 124, 129, 132) – **soul**    Noodles (pages 139, 144 ) – **movement**    Hotpots (pages 149, 153) – **gathering**
Sweet (pages 156, 159, 165) – **comfort**    Sauces and dressings (pages 166, 169 ) – **taste**    How to eat (pages 173, 176) – **eating**